FIGHTERS FOR FREEDOM:

Jefferson and Bolivar

FIGHTERS
FOR FREEDOM:
Jefferson and Bolivar

WRITTEN AND ILLUSTRATED BY

Hendrik Willem van Loon

DODD, MEAD & COMPANY
New York

Contents

THOMAS JEFFERSON

Contents

SIMON BOLIVAR

Illustrations

THOMAS JEFFERSON

SIMON BOLIVAR

THOMAS JEFFERSON

*The Serene Citizen from Monticello who
gave us an American Way of Thinking
and who gained World-Wide Renown
by his Noble Understanding
of that most Difficult of
all the Arts, The Art of
Living, as he felt that
it should be practiced
in the Republic of
which he was one of
the Founders.*

THOMAS JEFFERSON

I dedicate this volume
in old Friendship and Affection
to
RITA *and* STEPHEN BONSAL
who for a great many years
have been providing me with
those invaluable "intangibles"
which alone made it possible for me
to write about their "Uncle Tom"
as if I had really known him.

Chapter I.

A son is born to Colonel and Mrs. Peter Jefferson
of "Shadwell," Albemarle County, Virginia,
and he is called Thomas.

THIS IS THE STORY of a great American gentleman who was born in a remote part of the American wilderness but who lived to found a nation wherein, for the first time since the beginning of history, all men were guaranteed the right to life, to liberty and to the pursuit of happiness.

He came of good English stock, by which I do not mean that the Jeffersons were of noble descent. After he had become famous, several attempts were made to connect his family with the royal house of England, but Thomas Jefferson himself dismissed such claims as something unworthy of a citizen of the Republic, and though he wrote a great deal he never wasted any time on his family tree. He was too busy making his own career to bother about those of his ancestors.

When, therefore, I say that the Jeffersons came of good stock, I merely wish to imply that for several hundred years before they decided to migrate to the New World, they had belonged to a class of society which had set great store by its personal liberty. Those were the yeomen of medieval England, and in a great many respects

3

Thomas Jefferson was so much of an American counterpart of the old English yeomen that we can never hope to understand him nor the role he played in the founding of our republic unless we first of all form for ourselves a pretty clear idea of what that expression "yeoman" implied.

There are several theories about the original meaning of the word. There are those who connect it with just a plain and simple "young man," and in that case it would refer to the younger sons of a family of free landowners, who did not expect to inherit any of their father's estate and who would therefore take service with some lord and would serve him, just as a "young man" of today will hire himself out to a big corporation in the hope of afterwards becoming a vice-president or of holding some other important position.

But if we are still in the dark about the origin of the name, we are almost quite as ignorant about the way the class of these yeomen had come into existence, for they developed so gradually and normally that few people were aware of their existence until a long time after they had made their appearance. And once they had established themselves, they made it even harder for the historians to follow them by refusing to form a separate group, like the out-and-out nobles and the serfs and the out-and-out craftsmen and artisans.

To be a yeoman meant that one could do a great many things which the members of other classes of society could not do. For one thing, one had more freedom to move up and to move down.

4

One could be a small-scale landowner for example, and manage one's own farm, but one could also be a yeoman and at the same time act as a great lord's forester, like the yeoman you may remember from the Prologue to Chaucer's *Canterbury Tales*. The actual way in which one made one's living did not matter, as long as one retained one's personal liberty and had something in this world one could call one's own.

When the period for which a young yeoman had hired himself out was over, he could bid his master farewell and go wherever he wanted. Should he have been fortunate enough to have inherited his father's farm, no one could come and bother him or tell him what to do or take a single grain of corn away from him without due process of law.

His cottage, no matter how simple, how old, how poor or dilapidated, was his own and even the king himself could not cross the threshold of that edifice unless he had provided himself with an official warrant, duly signed by a regularly appointed magistrate who acted in the king's name. And though, taken as a whole, the yoo men were rarely very rich and usually belonged to the group of the small freeholders, they enjoyed a highly favorable position and one which was not held by any similar class in any other country of the late Middle Ages. For what William Pitt, the famous English statesman of the eighteenth century, said about them and their class was perfectly true, that "Even the poorest of them may, in his own cottage, bid defiance to all the forces of the Crown. That cottage may be frail; its roof may shake; the wind may blow through the seams of the walls. The storms may enter it. The rain may enter it. But the King of England cannot enter and all of the King's forces dare not cross the threshold of the ruined tenement of a free man."

And that was the truth. These yeomen might be poor, but they knew that they enjoyed certain "natural rights," as the men of our revolutionary days called them, and they set such great store by the possession of these "natural rights" that they were willing to uphold them and defend them at all costs—even at the cost of their lives.

Once you remember this, you have a key to the character of Thomas Jefferson. He was born in what was then the Far West of America and he did not set foot on European soil until he was in the middle of life. His people had been among the earlier settlers of Virginia and therefore he did not have a single direct contact with the land of his ancestors. But when the first of the Jeffersons decided to leave the old homestead in Wales and cross the ocean and begin all over again in a new world, he brought something with him much more useful than the money he had hidden in his trunk and the household goods stowed away in the hold of the vessel.

That was the tradition of freedom and independence which had always been the most cherished possession of the yeomen of England. And all through Jefferson's life you will find that, knowingly or unknowingly, he remained ever inspired by that old ideal which insisted that every man's house must be regarded as his castle and which stressed two virtues beyond all others, the virtue of self-reliance and therefore that of self-respect.

This need of being the master of his own fate, this joy in walking across such parcels of land as he could call his own, this dream of living the Good Life as best suited his own tastes and without interference from others were predominant traits in Thomas Jefferson's character, and this explains his dislike for large cities, for those vast clusters of houses where people are packed together like sardines, where no one can ever move a foot without being observed and criticized by his neighbors, and where man soon loses his identity and becomes what I have just called him, "a sardine in a box."

Now sardines in boxes, as you can observe for yourself the next time you have them for luncheon, do not lead a very exciting or a very glamorous existence. Someone with a gadget opens the box in which they were laid side by side and eats them. Jefferson never got over the feeling that such a fate was unworthy of a being created after the image of the Lord. He therefore felt strongly opposed to the accumulation of vast masses of people in big cities, just as he was against the accumulation of wealth in great big heaps that lay hidden in the strong-boxes of a few rich men; just as he was against letting too much authority be accumulated in the hands of a single man, be he a king, an emperor, a prelate or merely a county official. And just as he was against anything that might interfere in any way with a man's right to be himself.

Thomas Jefferson liked to consider the republic he had helped found as if it were a vast garden, the most wonderful garden in all the world, bestowed upon his fellow-

Americans by the kindness of the Good Lord and given unto them with the express understanding that they till it and work it according to their own desires, with the friendliest of feelings towards their neighbors and without casting jealous eyes upon the fields that lay on the other side of the stone fence. He himself was a living example of that philosophy which sees the beginning and end of all true happiness in the cultivation of one's own garden. He spent the eighty-three years he dwelled upon this earth as close as possible to the spot where his cradle had stood and where some day his grave was to be dug. Quite frequently important affairs of state took him away from his beloved little Monticello, but ever and again, the moment he was free, he hastened back to this "Little Hill" among the mountains of the Virginia wilderness. For there he could be himself and to be one's self seemed to him the highest form of human happiness—to be one's self, recognizing no other master than the Lord who had created this Paradise that man might enjoy the benefits therefrom but which man, in his fury and folly, was forever turning into a counterpart of the infernal regions, substituting tears for laughter, grief for joy and death for life.

April thirteenth (new style, April second, old style) was the day on which Thomas Jefferson was born and the year was 1743. The place where this event (an event not accompanied by the appearance of unexpected comets or other tokens of the unusual) occurred was a very simple house situated near a hamlet called Shadwell. This hamlet called Shadwell was in Albemarle County and

He knew the teeming, bare and overcrowded slums of Europe's big cities, where man soon loses his identity and becomes "a sardine in a box," and he hated them and considered them the cause of all human misery.

Albemarle County was so far removed from the rest of the world that nobody except a few Virginians knew of its existence.

If you want to find it on the map, look for a city called Charlottesville, which is the county seat and which you can locate by following the Rivanna River from where it leaves the James River on its own independent western course. There still is a post office which bears the name of Shadwell, but the house in which Thomas Jefferson saw the light of day is gone—as completely gone as any other farmhouse anywhere in America where somebody was a bit careless with a candle or forgot to bank a fire before closing the house for the night.

This disaster took place when Thomas Jefferson was twenty-six years old. It meant the destruction of his entire library. Of his law books, only one was saved. But he took it with the quiet acceptance of a true philosopher. The total cost of the books that went up in flames was more than a thousand dollars, but that did not interest him. "Would to God it had been the money," he wrote to a friend. "Then it had never cost me a sigh!"

His family at the time of his birth consisted of only his father and mother and two little girls. Afterwards there were to be a lot more, until the proud parents could boast of ten children in all, six of whom were girls. Two of them, both boys, died while still very young, but such a rate of mortality was quite normal for that day and age and in a region still inhabited by pioneers, for the frontier was hard on its mothers but even harder on its children. Only the very strong survived, but once they had safely

He also knew the wide open spaces of his own beloved land, where every man could have a bit of soil he could call his own and that he loved, for it would give the human race a chance to find freedom and independence and therefore happiness.

passed through the dangers of their first ten years (the wrong food, the wrong care, ignorant doctors and lack of the proper medicines), nothing could stop them and they were very apt to reach a ripe old age.

Thomas Jefferson was no exception. He died, comparatively hale and hearty (except for a few painful fingers, stiff with the gout), in his eighty-fourth year. When he was born, a great many people were still alive who with their own eyes had seen the great King Louis of France, who had been the resplendent incarnation of all that stood for royal pomp and tyranny. When he was carried to his grave, Napoleon, the incarnation of all that stood for imperial glory and tyranny, had already rested more than five years in his lonely grave on the island of St. Helena.

When young Master Jefferson had occasion to visit Charlottesville, he was taken there on a pillow on the back of a horse ridden by a black slave. When he died, so-called gravity railroads had been operated all along the Atlantic seaboard for more than ten years and the first steam-driven railroad was actually under construction. When he was born, serfdom was still being practiced in Europe and millions of peasants were little better off than the poor Blackamoors the New England sea captains imported from Africa and sold in the harbors of the South. Before he died, the movement to put an end to the disgrace of this form of human chattel had been seriously taken in hand and the generation which was born during the last ten years of his life was to put an end to that dreadful institution for good and all. When he was born, no man had ever soared like a bird, but when he died, only a few people well advanced in age remembered the first time a balloon had flown across the British Channel.

I might continue these comparisons for many pages to follow. When Thomas Jefferson went to Williamsburg to study law and prepare himself for a career in local politics, there surely was not a single one among the handful of settlers along the great American seaboard who had ever even dreamed of the possibility of turning the thirteen colonies away from the mother country. But when he died, the capital of a free and independent nation had long since been founded in another part of the Virginia wilderness. It had already been once destroyed by a foreign invader (the inevitable fate of all respectable capitals, then as now) and it had become a political center to which the rest of the world was beginning to pay serious, if quite unwilling, attention. And when he died, George Washington, the man without whose tenacity and perseverance and strength of character our nation would never have arisen triumphantly from its desperate and disheartening struggle for independence (and after whom that capital had been called), had been in his grave for twenty-seven years. Only one of his actual collaborators during the exciting days of the Declaration of Independence was then still alive. That was John Adams from Quincy, Massachusetts, the second President of the United States, but he survived his old personal friend and political enemy by only a couple of hours and then he, too, slipped quietly out of this life.

By the way, the day on which this happened was the fourth of July. And what a magnificent moment for a man who had as fine a sense of balance and timing as Thomas Jefferson, to make his final bow and take his departure!

All over the land the church bells were ringing to commemorate the birth of the new nation. The dying man was no longer interested. He had long since closed his account with that part of his career which had made him, almost against his will, one of the chief participants in the battle for freedom. That battle was over. It had been won a long time ago. Now only the future counted. Through the open windows came the soft buzzing of the industrious bees, tirelessly engaged upon their task of providing for the future. That was something he still could understand; this incessant labor for the benefit of generations as yet unborn; this devotion to a task that had to be accomplished for the common good; this eagerness to function—yes, that was the word—to function and make full use of one's abilities. For such was the law of God and all creation—that one must function to the best of one's abilities, not merely for one's self but also for the common good.

All of us must some day face the moment when we shall have to answer the question, "Has life been worth while? Has the sum total of happiness and the good things we have experienced surpassed the sum total of evil and unhappiness that has come our way?" We know very little about the inner secrets of the soul of even the best of our friends, but I think it is safe to say that few people have been able to answer that inquiry with as wholehearted a

14

"Yea" as Thomas Jefferson. And if he was among the fortunate ones, let us remember that it was not a matter of chance or accident, but that he had worked very hard to accomplish this purpose. He realized at a very early age that life is not something one accepts, as a child accepts a present that is handed to it from the Christmas tree. Life is a treasure we have got to cherish and we must tend it with everlasting care and devotion, so that when the hour comes when we must return it to the Donor, He will not be disappointed with the way we have taken care of it, for He is a severe judge in such matters and allows no excuses for indifference, negligence or careless workmanship.

Right here and while I have gone in for a rather heavy philosophical discussion, I might as well tell you that during the greater part of his life, Thomas Jefferson was bitterly attacked by his clerical neighbors. The ministers of the established church could not possibly approve of a politician who was an ardent advocate of a complete separation between Church and State. But such a separation was part of Thomas Jefferson's political program. He loved liberty in the widest sense of the word, and the idea that one particular sect could dominate all the others and tell them what they must believe and what not was as abhorrent to him as the prospect of having the power in England returned to a king who was a tyrant. Such a sovereign, on the other hand, would have been most heartily welcomed by the members of the duly established church and they showed their resentment of his "radical notions" (as they called them) by denouncing the occupant of the house on the Little Mountain as an agnostic, an atheist and an implacable enemy of God.

As a rule, Thomas Jefferson paid remarkably little attention to any kind of scandal that was being whispered against him. He had spent too many years of his life in official positions not to have come to an understanding of the tremendous harm that can be done to a person of outstanding abilities if he listens to "the envy of the small minds," as it expresses itself in that malicious rumor-mongering which is the way these "little minds" give expression to their envy. But in the end, when the vilifications the clerical gentlemen heaped upon him began to penetrate to the ears of his own children, he decided to define, once and for all, his attitude in regard to the teachings of Christ and his own feelings about the position the Church should hold in the community at large, and he wrote a little book which he called *The Philosophy of Jesus*, and which was afterwards published under the title of *Jefferson's Bible*.

I have read that book. If ever you come across a copy, please read it, too, for then you will agree with me that we need have no fear about what happened on that particular afternoon of the fourth of July of the year 1826 when Jefferson went to hear his final sentence. I doubt whether the tired old gentleman was obliged to wait as long as ordinary mortals. Most likely even St. Peter had walked down the road a bit to welcome so distinguished a visitor. I don't know, of course, what they said to each other. But Thomas Jefferson, remembering the days of his childhood and his training at Sunday School, may have

16

felt that on such occasions it was better to bring at least a few documents with which to bear out one's statement that one had not completely wasted one's time on earth.

"If it please you, my good St. Peter, here I have a few old papers—just odds and ends—and these will perhaps show you that I have done the best according to my lights. Here, for example, is a document about human rights. I wrote it one hot day in July of 1776. And here is a little book I once composed to refute a good many rather absurd statements about my so-called lack of religion, and here is still something else about public education and about freedom of conscience, but perhaps you had better look at them for yourself."

And then I can see the saintly old keeper of the Pearly Gates as he quietly pushes these papers back into the pockets of that old and well-worn brown coat, which Jefferson wore until the day of his death, and I can see him as he takes his guest gently by the arm and tells him, "Such evidence may be of use in a human court of justice, my dear Thomas Jefferson, for there you have to struggle with the intricacies of the legal mind which is so apt to take the letter for the law. But it is not needed here, where we read straight into the hearts of all men. So throw these bits of paper away or burn them or just forget about them, and, meanwhile, come right in. There is Someone here Who wants to see you and Who wants to see you very much, and He is not in the least interested in what you have written about life. He only cares about the way you lived it."

Chapter II.

How young Master Thomas spent his childhood
days under the happiest of circumstances, until
the sudden death of his father forced him to
assume grave personal responsibilities at
an age when most boys are just
beginning to think of going
to college and enjoying
themselves.

THE JEFFERSONS, when they had crossed the ocean (a tremendous adventure during the latter half of the seventeenth century), had not in any way ceased to be the sort of people they had always been in the Old World. They had quietly stuck to the middle of the road. They had neither grown very rich nor had they suffered the fate of so many other immigrants who, once they had been cut loose from their old moorings, had grown slovenly and careless, with the inevitable result that they had lost their possessions and had slipped into the class of common day-laborers, obliged to hire out to others for their daily bread, whiskey and molasses.

Within the realm of both religion and politics, the Jeffersons had never taken sides, preferring to be left alone and to attend to their own business, whether it be of this world or the next. Like the majority of the other colonists, they were very busy trying to make a living out of a virgin soil and therefore perfectly willing to let the King be the King and to let the Archbishop be the Archbishop, provided those dignitaries ruled according to the laws of the land and took no liberties with those highly valued privileges which the yeomen had succeeded in gaining during the course of a great many centuries.

Nor did those immigrants in any way object to being considered and to being called "colonials." Provided again that such rights as had been bestowed upon the settlers in the New World by the different chartered companies, which owned those vast tracts of land along the western seaboard of the Atlantic, were duly respected by the governors who represented the Royal Majesty in the New World, they were quite contented with their lot and asked neither favors nor questions. Indeed, it took an almost incredible amount of tactless arrogance, pigheadedness and plain, ordinary stupidity to arouse these patient colonials to a point where they had no other choice but to arise in open rebellion against their German-minded King and his dull-witted ministers.

But at the time Thomas Jefferson was born, in 1743, the mere notion of a move for independence from the mother country was still something so utterly fantastic that it had never entered anybody's mind. Redress of certain real and imaginary evils might be an occasional subject of conversation but the idea of a formal separation from the mother country was never mentioned.

Virginia, founded a few years before the New Netherlands had been established at the mouth of the Hudson
River and thirteen years before the Pilgrims had settled
down in New England, was in many respects the most
comfortable part of the American world in which an immigrant from the Old World could hope to look for a new
home.

Curiously enough, the colony's prosperity was due to a
weed. This weed had been known to the people of the
latter half of the sixteenth century as the *herba sancta
indorum,* or "the divine herb of the Indies." It had found
its way to Spain in the year 1558 and it had traveled to
the Old World as part of a collection of supposedly "useful products" which had been gathered together in Mexico by order of King Philip II of Spain. Until then, of
course, the Spaniards had looked upon the New World as
a profitable field of plunder, but as the gold supply
was beginning to get exhausted, His Majesty's ministers
had suggested that the newly acquired territories be sci-
entifically explored, investigated and catalogued, to see
whether they might not reveal some new agricultural
products which could be grown in Europe and which
would prevent the European peasants from starving to
death, at the same time adding to the Royal revenues.

Don Francisco Fernandes, the head of this survey expedition, had sent a few specimens of the mysterious "Indian herb" to Seville, without knowing exactly what
Europe would ever be able to do with it. The Indians of
Mexico used to dry the leaves of this plant, which the
natives called "tabacco" (an Indian word, like "potato"

and "tomato" which soon got incorporated into practically all European languages). They used to put it into a
bowl with a long clay stem to it and they would set fire to
the mess and inhale the fumes, thereby, so they claimed,
getting themselves into a state of happy excitement,
an excitement which allowed them to forget all their
worldly worries and to let themselves be transported into
the realm of the blessed.

The European explorers had of course eagerly tried to
partake of this pleasure, that they too might forget their
miseries for a few moments (the life of an explorer is
rarely a happy one), but all they had experienced was a
case of horrible nausea.

The French ambassador in Portugal, a certain Mon-
sieur Jean Nicot, having heard about the wonderful qualities of tobacco as a means of killing pain, had secretly got
hold of a few of the seeds and had forwarded them to his
royal mistress, Queen Catherine, of the illustrious Italian
House of the Medici, but of very unhappy memory, as
you will discover when you read French history.

Her Majesty, however, cannot be held responsible for
the spreading of the smoking habit across the continent
of Europe. Her ambassador in Portugal derived some
benefits from his activities, on behalf of the new weed, for
nowadays when little boys hide themselves behind the
barn and try their first cigarette, their papa, giving them
a fresh green apple, will tell them that it is the *nicotine*
(the poisonous alkaloid that lies hidden in those leaves)
which has been the cause of their dreadful seasickness
and that they had better give nicotine a wide berth if they

hope to grow up into strong and sturdy men.

After these initial failures, it looked very much as if the "Divine Herb of the Indies" was doomed to a speedy oblivion as far as the people of Europe were concerned, or at best might survive in the apothecary shops. For a learned pharmacist had meanwhile discovered that if you boiled these leaves long enough they would produce a sirupy substance, and when that was given to a patient he either died right away or recovered because he was of such a sound constitution that nothing could kill him short of being hit over the head with a battle-axe.

The tobacco plant, therefore, seemed a complete failure until by chance it found its way to England. The sober-minded Britishers, who had stronger stomachs than the Spaniards and the French, could actually smoke the stuff and derived great enjoyment from the experience. Ralph Lane, the first governor of Virginia, was also the first Englishman to smoke a pipe of tobacco and live to tell the tale. He and Sir Francis Drake interested Sir Walter Raleigh in their tobacco proposition and Sir Walter is said to have become such an inveterate smoker that he asked for a pipe of tobacco just before he had his head chopped off. This was good advertising for the virtues of tobacco as a nerve soother, for Sir Walter must have been very much annoyed at the prospect of losing his head as the only reward for his many years of faithful and painful service to good Queen Bess.

To make a long story just a little longer, once the people of Northern Europe had got the taste of the wicked weed in their mouths and in their nostrils, nothing could stop them from smoking their pipes of tobacco, except in Turkey and Russia, where anybody found with tobacco on his breath was at once beheaded. But everywhere else the people were soon clamoring for their pipes and when it was discovered that the soil of Virginia was ideally suited for the raising of *nicotiana tabacum,* that part of the New World soon became the center of the tobacco trade. So much so, that just as in the New Netherlands the skin of the beaver had been the "unit of trade," by means of which the settlers had dealt with each other and with the home country, it was the bale of tobacco which in Virginia took the place of ordinary currency and indicated by its abundance or its absence the wealth and social standing of its owner.

And it was not merely the government officials and the ordinary merchants who were paid in tobacco, but even ministers were rewarded for their holy services by so many pounds of tobacco per annum. It was quite typical of the Jeffersons and an indication of their sense of independence that they did not go in for tobacco raising but made a specialty of raising wheat.

Meanwhile, once in America, they were obliged to do as the Americans did and that meant that they must keep slaves. They did not like this. They detested the institution, but what else could they do? Someone had to work their fields and who was there to do this except the patient and powerful black man imported from overseas? This is a most unfortunate subject and I wish that I could avoid it, but I can't, for eventually slavery led up to that ghastly massacre which we now call the Civil War, during which our nation lost more than a million of its youngest and most promising citizens. And here is a question which even today puzzles a great many people— why did Thomas Jefferson, who declared before the whole world that all men are born free and are equally entitled to life, liberty and the pursuit of happiness—why did he, for most of his life, keep almost a hundred slaves on his own plantation? Why didn't he set them free, since he sincerely believed that all men are indeed born free and are entitled to life and liberty? I am afraid that he would have found it very hard to answer that question, for way down deep in his heart he felt just the way all of us do to-day—that there is absolutely no excuse for one half of humanity keeping the other half in bondage and treat-ing their fellow human-beings as if they were so much cattle, which the owner could whip or even kill at his own convenience.

But when Jefferson lived, he was practically alone in his views. The vast majority of the people all over the world took the existence of the Human Slave just as much for granted as we of today take the existence of the Iron Slave for granted. By the Iron Slave, I mean, of course, the machine which a century and a half ago took the place of the Human Slave and which today does practi-cally all the work that has to be done to feed the human race and to keep it warm and comfortable.

When you read the ancient Greek and Roman philos-ophers, you discover that even in those remote times there were quite a number of thoughtful and considerate men who maintained grave doubts about the moral aspects of a system which then condemned almost seventy per cent of the human race to spend its days "slaving" for someone else, without the slightest hope of ever achieving any kind of personal freedom of either thought or action—without a chance of raising a family of its own—without a right to its own children (which could be sold at any moment, as today the puppies in a dog-kennel can be sold)—without a home of its own or any worldly possessions which it could call its own.

But what could they do about it? That was the eternal question which no one had ever been able to answer. For suppose you told these millions of slaves (most of them prisoners of war, acquired during the endless campaigns of the Romans against the wild people of Northern Europe, Western Asia and North Africa)—suppose you told them that they were free and could go wherever they liked. What would happen then? It was undoubtedly a most commendable idea but it also was completely impractical, for it would have meant the collapse of the economic, and therefore of the social fabric of the state. Everybody would have starved to death for lack of agricultural laborers and the people of the cities would have risen in revolt, as they themselves had long since lost the habit of working a farm. The profitable factories of the Rhine Valley (the Detroit region of the ancient world) would have been obliged to close their doors. The domestic servants would have walked out and nobody would any longer have had a cook or a waiter or a gardener. All the craftsmen, the carpenters, bakers, butchers, plumbers and candlestick-makers were slaves and not a stroke of work would have been done until a new race of free carpenters, bakers, butchers, plumbers and candle-stick-makers had been developed, and that would have taken a great deal of time.

After all, one could not very well expect a whole class of society to commit suicide for the benefit of an ideal. Wherefore, though the more enlightened part of humanity disapproved, slavery continued, in one form or another, until well within the days of our own grandfathers, and even recently there has been an attempt to revive a new but just as cruel form of slavery in Europe. And when, as well you may, you hear people criticize Thomas Jefferson as a man who did not live up to his own principles of "freedom for all people" and who remained the owner of a hundred black slaves while working hard to set four million white people free from the infinitely milder bondage in which they were held by the mother country, remember that he had practically no other choice. Privately he did the best he could by quietly allowing as many of his own servants as possible to gain their liberty, but he was terribly handicapped by the fact that society at large greatly disapproved of such a procedure. Also, he had learned that those who hope to accomplish much should remain faithful to the wise old principle of "One thing at a time."

And so he began at home. He did his best, first of all, to rid Virginia of the wicked nightmare of human slavery. But when he realized that the opposition was still too strong to allow him to accomplish anything practical, he did the next best thing by setting an excellent example of treating those unfortunate creatures like human beings and he tried to persuade his neighbors to do likewise. And we know (from the comments of a great many of his contemporaries) that the Blackamoors who worked for him inside his home and on his fields were a contented and happy lot and regarded themselves much more as his children than as his servants. If they showed any particular ability for some craft, they were trained to become masons or carpenters or ironworkers, for Monticello was so far removed from the center of civilization that everything, both inside and outside of the house, had to be done by local labor. And with a race with which kindness has always gone much further than with any other, Thomas Jefferson's "personal approach," consisting of gentle manners and good humor and a deep sense of gaiety, achieved miracles.

Indeed, during his last and bitter days, when it seemed that his generosity and hospitality to both strangers and friends and his faith in the honesty of his fellow-men had carried him to the verge of bankruptcy, so that everything he owned would have to be sold to settle his debts, it was not the master himself who was worried by the prospect of seeing his beloved Monticello auctioned off to the highest bidder. The master was too old to care much either one way or the other. He had lived such a full life that it did not really matter very much whether he died in his own home or in that of a friend. Things were bound to happen in this world as they would happen, and a man of "life upright" did not let himself be bowed down by adverse circumstances nor would he fear the blows that fate or ill-fortune might bring. But the poor slaves were in despair. "Where," so they asked each other, "where shall we ever again find so good and kind a master, so truly a father to his children?"

This Thomas Jefferson, I find, is a very difficult person to write about. Even in his old age he will remain as elusive as a young colt. You can never ask him to stand still and to stay still for more than a few moments at a time. Being blessed with an irrepressible inquisitiveness, he will be forever galloping off on some new track. Everything pertaining to the vast domain of human experience he considered a fit object of investigation. Had he been merely a statesman (a profession which at heart he rather distrusted and disliked) or a soldier (a career for which he had small natural aptitude) or a plantation owner or a writer upon almost every subject between heaven and earth (being the author of treatises on soil improvement, as well as the compiler of a Bible of his own), I could easily enough take him in hand and I would be able to tell you just exactly what he did in every given year of his long and useful life. But he was always busy with at least a dozen things at the same time.

While administering his broad acres, he was writing political pamphlets. While representing his country abroad, he collected vegetables and plants that might be grown profitably on the other side of the ocean, and copied blueprints for new kinds of machinery and consulted engineers about housing projects. While trying to make a success of his new experiment in self-government, he would draw up elaborate plans for educating the kind of boys and girls that would have to live in a country wherein the citizens must now rule themselves. And when finally he had bade farewell to the activities of a public career, he did not merely settle down to the peaceful pursuits of a retired statesman but spent all his waking hours upon the project of his "ideal community," wherein man would be the master of his own fate.

And in between he kept himself occupied with the more immediate problem of bringing up his own children, with inventing dumbwaiters so that the food and wine he served his guests would reach the dining-room table at exactly the right temperature, and with keeping his fiddle fingers sufficiently practiced so that, if the occasion demanded it, he could supply the company with the right kind of music for either a song or a dance, for he strongly believed in a cheerful and merry life.

However, I promised that I would tell you enough about his life to make you understand why many of us regard him as the greatest American of all time and books —alas—can only be so many pages and no more. I shall, therefore, do my best to stick to the narrow road of the actual events in Thomas Jefferson's life and there will be no further detours, or as few as possible, while writing about a man whose mind was so versatile that he himself was the most marvelous of "wanderers" in the best sense of the word.

The father of our hero, like most of the yeomen of his day and age, had one great ambition. He wanted to found a family and he wanted to leave his children a little better off than he himself had been during the days of his early youth. He therefore bade farewell to the tidewater region (the region nearest to the coast), where all the better pieces of land had long since been occupied, and moved into the tablelands of the interior of Virginia, where he had a better chance to create a small semi-independent domain of his own.

He began in the year 1735 by staking out a claim for a thousand acres along the banks of the Rivanna River. He meant to specialize in wheat, for the tobacco growers of the seaboard had to eat and his thirty slaves (you see, he was a comparatively poor man when he started out) could take care of that much wheat and of everything else he needed for the daily maintenance of his family.

The older Jefferson was not only a man of enormous physical strength and very distinguished appearance, but he seems to have been a true gentleman of great personal charm, for he was on the most friendly terms with all of his neighbors and he had established a cordial relationship with that famous Colonel William Randolph, who, during the middle of the eighteenth century, was the recognized leader of the social and economic life of the colony. Indeed, the two men were so sincerely attached to each other that when Peter Jefferson needed a site for a new home, it was the mighty Colonel Randolph who let him have four hundred of his acres in exchange for a mere bowl of Arak punch. This, of course, was a joke, as Arak punch in the Virginia of the eighteenth century was as common as milk in a modern nursery.

Soon afterwards, Colonel Jefferson had still further allied himself with the most powerful dynasty of Virginia landowners by actually marrying into the Randolph family. His wife's name was Jane. She had been born in London, in a parish called Shadwell, and in honor of his young bride, Peter Jefferson called his newly-built house Shadwell. It was a very simple, clapboard affair, but it was only a beginning, for Peter Jefferson hoped to be able to replace it by something much more substantial just as soon as his finances would allow such a step.

Colonel Randolph died six years after his daughter's marriage. He had made his friend, Peter Jefferson, his executor and the latter, in order to be near the premises, moved his family to a plantation named Tuckahoe, situated on the banks of the James River, a few miles above the city of Richmond.

Afterwards, Thomas Jefferson used to tell of this migration, which was one of the earliest of his childhood recollections. He was three years old at that time, but being a bright child he never forgot that glorious trip, strapped to a pillow on the back of the horse of one of the family retainers.

It was therefore at Tuckahoe and not at Shadwell that Thomas Jefferson spent the first and most impressionable years of his life. It was a peaceful and happy existence. Private tutors taught him all a young gentleman of independent means was supposed to know and there was no better schooling for a lively young boy than a plantation of a century and a half ago, which was a world in and by and for itself.

Through his mother (who was a Randolph, and please

don't forget it!) he belonged to the "inner circle" of the colonial life of Virginia. And so all was set for an agreeable and profitable career as a successful plantation owner when suddenly, in the year 1757, Colonel Peter Jefferson was taken sick and died. He was only fifty years old but as a royal surveyor (he published the first maps of the colony of Virginia) Peter Jefferson had lived the rough life of the frontier and had experienced all kinds of hardships, some of which may have undermined his health.

Afterwards, his duties as colonel of the Albemarle militia (the Indians were still quite a problem and often attacked the settlers), as a justice of the peace of a frontier county and a delegate to the House of Burgesses had probably made him overtax his strength. But like most other physical giants (it was said of him that he could set two hogsheads of tobacco, each weighing a thousand pounds, upright at the same time), he had probably lived under the delusion that he was not made of ordinary human clay and that therefore he could safely disregard all the ordinary laws of health.

He now discovered that he had been wrong, but it was too late to do anything about it. And so his loving neighbors carried him reverently to his grave and wondered whether there was anybody else in the community who could take his place, for their Colonel had not only been a great leader of men but while most of the members of his caste had been out-and-out conservatives, who never —for Heaven's sake!—wanted anything changed, Peter Jefferson had been quite a liberal. Especially in carrying out his duties as justice of the peace, he had often shown that his real sympathies lay with the poor and the disinherited rather than with the rich and powerful, and his verdicts had usually been on the side of the oppressed.

This tendency towards what we would now call a democratic view of life he had already bestowed upon his young son. But there was one other quality which young Thomas had inherited from his father. All during his life, Colonel Peter Jefferson had taught his son that he must never let someone else do for him what he could do for himself. It was a habit which stuck to the author of the Declaration of Independence until the end of his days. Even when he was in his eighties, along with his friend and enemy, John Adams, he was still in the habit of getting up early in the morning to make his own fire, and if it could possibly be done, he took care of his own horse, for his horse, to him, was a personal friend who must be treated with great regard.

But then there was something in the educational methods of two centuries ago which we might well study and to a certain extent try to imitate. There were lots of things the boys of those long-ago days did not know. But at a very early age they had been taught to take care of themselves and they felt a sense of responsibility towards themselves and their families which is almost completely absent in our own day. Think of this whenever you feel that life may have been a little too hard on you.

Thomas Jefferson was fourteen years old when his father's death made him the head of the household, the manager of quite a large estate, the protector of the interests of his mother and his brothers and sisters and the responsible owner of three score slaves. But this was so common an occurrence in the year of 1757 that nobody seemed in the least surprised that he made a success of the job that was so unexpectedly forced upon him.

The older men of the community welcomed him as an equal. The older women thought that this nice-looking, good-humored and well-to-do boy might some day make an excellent husband for one of their daughters. And so life went on as pleasantly as before, except that Jane Jefferson now felt that she must be both a father and a mother to her brood and be it said to that good lady's everlasting glory that she more than lived up to her promise.

All of us owe a lot to Thomas Jefferson, who gave us our Republic, or—if you think that that is too much praise for a single individual—who assisted so nobly in giving us our independence. But we also owe a debt of deep gratitude to Jane Jefferson, to the faithful mother who spent the two decades after her husband's death in giving form and shape to her oldest son's character. For it was from her that he derived many of his most outstanding qualities—his gaiety and his ability to get along with almost every kind of human being, without ever losing sight of the fact that there must be a certain "distance" between himself and those a little less favored by nature, if both of them were expecting to function to the best of their abilities.

By which, of course, I do not mean that Jefferson was ever capable of an act of snobbery. Heaven forbid! He

At an age when other children still played their games, little Tommy Jefferson was already managing the family estate.

was the most natural of men and every kind of pose was foreign to his nature. But since he respected all other people, he also expected to be treated with due ceremony. There was nothing of the hail-fellow-well-met about him. No one outside of a small circle of pleasant friends ever dreamed of calling Mr. Thomas Jefferson plain Tom. They would as soon have saluted His Excellency, the first President of the Republic, with a loud, "How are you, George?" as they would have brought themselves to Mr. Jefferson's attention by shouting, "Hey there, Tom!" Not because the Washingtons or the Jeffersons or the Adamses ever worried about their "dignity." They were not in the need of doing so because they had it. The word "dignity" has the same root as "dainty" and shows that a person observes a certain "daintiness" in the choice of his friends and his manners and customs and habits.

And that quality of a sincere "daintiness" is dealing with all the problems of life, which young Thomas had undoubtedly acquired from both his paternal and maternal ancestors, cropped up in all sorts of unexpected nooks and corners of his character. In an age of notoriously vulgar habits in the matter of eating and drinking (cooking in the frontier kitchens was the equivalent of frying and drunkenness was the order of the day), Thomas Jefferson was famous for his delicate taste in everything he allowed to reach his table. Being a person who profoundly detested the whiskey and rum-guzzling of his time, he specialized in wines and made great efforts to turn his neighbors from tipsy grog-swillers into delicate wine-drinkers by starting vineyards of his own and by sending abroad for the right kinds of grapes with which to improve his own vintage.

As for the food he ate, it had, of course, to be simple but it must be very well prepared. He loathed the meals of which his contemporaries partook with the gusto of half-starved bears. He never cared to sit through a meal of ten or fifteen courses (and these were by no means the exception a century and a half ago), but was contented with one or two dishes that were the proud products of the black-skinned chef who presided over the kitchen in Monticello's basement.

This refined taste in the matter of food did not go unobserved by his neighbors, and Patrick Henry, whose background had been very different from that of Mr. Jefferson, made sound political capital out of the fact that the high-and-mighty squire of Monticello was at heart more of a Frenchman than an American in the choice of his food and therefore undoubtedly must be also lacking in those other staunch virtues which were supposed to make an American superior to a subject of King Louis.

There is still another item—often overlooked—in which Thomas Jefferson was quite unique among the run of his fellow-politicians, then or now. I have already mentioned how, from his mother, he had inherited a sincere love of music. The Greeks were right when they made music one of the most important items on their program of education. They did not expect everybody to become a concert virtuoso, but to them a man who could not hold his own in a choir or did not know his way about on at least one instrument remained a "barbarian." As it was well nigh impossible to transport a harpsichord all the way to either Tuckahoe or Monticello (there were no roads, everything had to be carried on the back of a mule), Jefferson had to content himself with a violin. He owned several quite passable fiddles. He played on them until a broken arm (a horseback accident) made it very awkward for him to handle a bow, but all during his life he used to send to London for the latest compositions that had been published there, as his taste went out towards simple English ballads rather than to the more complicated works of the Italians and the French.

Today, I am afraid, that it would be very difficult for a man to be elected to the Presidency if it were known that he took an active part in music, for people would suspect that he did not devote all his working hours to business of State.

In giving credit to his mother for all these pleasant and amiable characteristics, I must not overlook the contributions the father made towards the intellectual and social perfections of his son, a few of which I have already mentioned. From his father, young Thomas inherited his size, for he stood well over six feet two, but whereas his father had put on weight during the latter part of his life, the son ever retained the slimness of his mother. Also it was from his father that he acquired his love for details, his meticulous habit of keeping everything in its right place, his respect for well-balanced bank accounts and his insistence that all things be done in order and with decency.

After he had gone to the White House and had become

an object of hatred and derision for all those who feared that his love for the common man might deprive them of some of their inherited riches, Thomas Jefferson was denounced as a slovenly buffoon who did not know how to dress, who received foreign ambassadors in a dirty old dressing-gown, and who was a disgrace to the elegant traditions that should prevail at the executive mansion of the rich and powerful United States. But just as in the case of Abraham Lincoln, who was called an "uncouth yokel" until the day of his death by those who regarded him as a dangerous demagogue, there was very little truth in such accusations.

It is undoubtedly true that President Jefferson positively refused to be driven in state to the Capitol when he had to go there to take his oath of office, preferring to proceed on foot. But this apparent disregard of what was then considered "good form" may have been due quite as much to the abominable state of the roads of our national capital (up to the end of the Civil War, even Pennsylvania Avenue was either a trough filled with dust or a quagmire) as to any deliberate desire for rather ostentatious simplicity. And none of the distinguished visitors who ever came to either Washington or Monticello have failed to inform us how greatly they were impressed by the exquisite courtesy with which they were received by America's foremost citizen, and without exception they have borne witness to the excellent table and cellar of their host and to the charm that prevailed within the walls of the Executive Mansion while Thomas Jefferson was the nation's official host.

Yes, Thomas Jefferson, with such a father and such a mother, started out with quite unusual advantages, but he also worked very hard to make his talents go as far as he could. For in addition to many other virtues, he had a deep and sincere sense of obligation. It was up to him to fulfill his father's ambition to bestow upon his family certain honors that should not be unworthy of the best traditions of his beloved Virginia.

By and large, the world has come to agree that this fourteen-year-old boy more than lived up to the promise he had made to his father.

Chapter III.

*How force of circumstances, rather than choice,
gradually made Thomas Jefferson drift into
local politics, and the issues which were
beginning to divide the colonists
into mutually hostile camps.*

IN AMERICA it was not customary, as it was among the leading classes of England, to leave all of one's property to the oldest son, so that the estate would be held together. Peter Jefferson, with his democratic leanings, had therefore bequeathed his smaller estate, called Snowdon, to his younger son, Randolph. But the bulk of the estate, including Shadwell, which meanwhile had been changed into a comfortable residence, went to Thomas. The girls were expected to marry, in which case, as a matter of course, their brother Thomas would not only make them happy with his blessing, but would also provide them with a suitable dowry.

As for the widowed mother, she would stay on at Shadwell and continue to run the household, for the other children were still very young (Randolph was a mere baby) and they needed a home.

Colonel Jefferson had not been in a position to acquire

much of an education. Although legally these men of the New World were still considered British colonials, they were also becoming sufficiently American in their outlook upon life to insist that their offspring be given a better chance at getting ahead than they themselves had enjoyed. Therefore young Thomas, while still quite a small boy, had been packed off to the home of a Scotch clergyman, where he had been thoroughly drilled in the principles of the Latin language. After his father's death, his guardians sent him to a boarding-school, this time conducted by a minister who belonged to the Church of England, and there he added Greek to what he already knew about the Latin vernacular.

Young Thomas took to these studies as a duck takes to water, and when he was quite old he confessed that if the choice between his father's estate and a thorough knowledge of the classical tongues had been put before him, he would have chosen the latter. Now if he had been a mere schoolboy when he said this, we would have known what to think. Little Tommy Jefferson was trying to curry favor with his teachers and what better way than by telling them how much he loved his *amo—amas—amat*. But as I just said, he made this statement late in life, long after he had ceased to care what his masters might think of him.

He therefore must have felt that way, and we can understand this attitude if we remember what it meant, two hundred years ago, to be a good classical scholar. It made one a member of a sort of International Brotherhood of cultivated people. Of course, there was no such brotherhood in the sense that today there are Brotherhoods of Locomotive Engineers and Free-masons and Hod Carriers and College Professors, but all the people everywhere who had gone through that same classical course of training had a bond in common which gave the world at large a feeling of intellectual unity which since then has completely disappeared, and more is the pity!

Now, of course, almost any boy of fourteen (unless he has absolutely no interest in his school work) will occasionally feel a strong desire to become a famous scholar, to learn all the languages there are (he rarely suspects how many there are) and to know every department of the sciences, so that he may qualify as a chemist as well as an engineer and become in a way the recognized and universal genius of the ages. As a rule, that ambition (fortunately for our teachers and for their pupils, too) does not last more than a few weeks or at most a few months. But in the case of young Thomas, it continued until the end of his life, and as soon as it was discovered that small private schools could no longer teach him anything, he was hastened to the College of William and Mary in Williamsburg, that he might there bring his education to such perfection as the colony had to offer.

The College of William and Mary had been founded in 1693, just fifty-seven years after Harvard. That made it the second oldest university on the northern half of the American continent, for in the southern half it would have been looked down upon as a mere upstart, as academies and colleges in Central and South America had been founded as early as the first half of the sixteenth century. From our present-day point of view, William and Mary was still a rather primitive affair, but it was the best the colonists had to offer to their children and Thomas Jefferson considered himself very fortunate indeed that he had such an excellent training-school so near at hand. And when he left he had acquired, among other things, a sound knowledge of the Latin, the Greek, the French, the Spanish and the Italian languages and had even (Heaven only knows how) acquired a few of the rudiments of some of the sciences.

When I use the expression "sound knowledge," I do not mean that all he knew of these foreign tongues was a few sentences, carefully culled from a convenient copybook. No, he could handle all of them with such ease that he could converse in them with both fluency and elegance, so that during the many years he represented our country in Europe he was able to deal with foreign statesmen without ever being under the obligation of using an interpreter.

In addition to his vast philological labors, he sweated away so industriously at mathematics and every other kind of science which might come in handy while administering his estate that within fifteen years after his father's death he had increased his holdings from a mere 1900 to 5000 acres, not counting almost double that amount which came to him after his father-in-law's death. That estate, however, was so heavily mortgaged that it brought him more trouble than happiness. All the same, it took a lot of practical administrative ability to handle such a small kingdom, so far removed from the center of

The best university in the world—a boy lost in an interesting book in front of an open fire.

civilization, but Jefferson was an excellent manipulator of figures and during his college years he had learned all the latest tricks in accounting and bookkeeping.

And what of the other—the so-called cultural activities—which are supposed to count so heavily in our own day and age? Well, Jefferson was neither a grind nor a prig and he carefully attended all the parties to which he was invited. More than that, he not only went but he always tried to make himself agreeable and useful, playing the necessary music whenever the company felt inclined to dance. Also, like a normal lad, he quite often fell in love and just as frequently he fell out again. But he most carefully avoided those pitfalls (much more common then than now) which might have made him lose his last penny over a midnight gambling table or get mixed up in a drunken brawl, settled after the custom of the time by some such absurdity as a duel.

He did, however, take a very active part in all kinds of sport. He loved horses and continued to ride horseback until almost the very end of his long life, but he never risked any of his money on horse races, knowing that that is one of the most dependable ways in which to lose not only your hat and coat but also your shirt. By the same token, while he played every known game, he did not like to play for stakes. He was a most welcome guest at the home of the Honorable Francis Fauquier, Lieutenant-Governor of Virginia, but he let His Excellency, who was famous as a most reckless gambler, shuffle the cards and roll the dice while he himself stood by or found some more congenial amusement in another part of the executive mansion.

This could not always have been easy, as it is very difficult for a young man, when invited by his elders to sit in at a friendly game, to answer, "No, thank you. I had rather not." It takes both tact and a knowledge of the world to make such a reply without hurting anybody's feelings. That Jefferson was able to do this while still in his teens shows that he had had an excellent schooling in the civilities of life, as indeed he had.

There was still one more thing he did not do, for which he drew the attention upon himself of a society which lived in a constant haze of tobacco smoke. Thomas Jefferson never used snuff nor did he ever puff at a pipe. I think I know the reason. He was, as I have already pointed out, very partial to good food and he had learned at an early age that smoking is very apt to dull one's taste for the more delicate pleasures of the table. He therefore made his choice. He did not moralize about it but he himself stuck to his food and wine and let the tobacco go.

And so the busy years of his university life came to an end and Thomas Jefferson was faced with the choice of a career, for just administering a plantation was not considered enough of an outlet for a young man of his unusual talents. He had a profound distrust of oratory as such, but since the law offered the best chance for advancement, he decided to become a lawyer (but as much as possible without the oratory). In 1763 and in his twenty-first year, he entered the law offices of one George Wythe, of the town of Williamsburg, and there he copied letters, made out wills and conveyances and did all those odd jobs which were then considered the equal of four years at a regular law school. Having given evidence of a sufficient amount of industry and common sense to plead a case of his own, he was duly admitted to the Bar of Virginia and thereupon practiced law for seven years.

At the end of this period, he said, "Enough is enough!" and withdrew from the courthouse and from the foolish arguments in futile cases, which did not interest him in the least. And never after that happy moment did he again have anything to do with the business of settling other people's quarrels for the benefit of his own pocket.

He was then still quite a young man. His father's inheritance had greatly prospered under his careful management. His law practice had doubled the income he derived from his plantations, for he was quick-witted and could, if necessary, split hairs as well as the next one. But why should he engage in a profession that was not at all to his taste? He was good-looking, amiable, rich, of an excellent family, and the future looked bright and rosy. But in every man's life there seem to be turns over which he has little or no control and because he does not quite know why such things have happened to him, he tells himself that it was Fate which took a hand, and I suppose it is as good an excuse as any other.

Well, Fate gave Thomas Jefferson exactly the kind of wife he had always hoped for. Her name was Martha Wayles Skelton. She was six years younger than her husband and, according to all who knew her, a woman of great charm and beauty. But Fate also decided that he should lose his adored Martha after only ten years of a completely congenial companionship. And Fate also decided that of the six children that were born to the couple, only two girls were to survive beyond infancy. Fate therefore, in one respect, was very harsh in dealing with this young man whom she had favored in almost every other respect. He had loved his Martha so devotedly that he could never persuade himself to marry again. Though in the course of his career he met all the most fascinating women of both the Old and the New World, he was polite but never showed any interest in them beyond the sending of a civil note or a bunch of flowers. That part of life was over for him, and it was over for good and all. He still devoted a great deal of his time to the education of his two daughters, but the prospect of a happy domestic existence of his own had come to an end almost before it had begun.

However, after he had recovered from his first uncontrollable grief, Jefferson realized that he would have to find something to make up for his feeling of loss and emptiness, and that is how he gradually drifted into politics. He was not by any means what we sometimes call a "born politician." He was a man of such strong principles that he felt no love whatsoever for the game of politics as such. At the same time, certain things had to be done, if the world were not to come to a complete standstill, and since politics in the better sense of the word means "getting things done," he let himself first of all be chosen a Justice of the Peace of his own county and afterwards he accepted a seat in the House of Burgesses of the colony of Virginia.

These offices did not demand much of his time and nei-

In those days a gentleman could still amuse himself play-
ing the violin.

ther did they take him far away from home. He could still
attend to the affairs of his little private domain and he
could supervise the education of his little girls. In the eve-
nings, when he was not busy with his accounts, he could
play the fiddle or read his favorite Latin authors or write
letters to almost any man of importance in any part of the
world. On the whole, a pleasant enough life and one
which, of his own choice, he would hardly have given up
for any other. But all the plans of everybody in the New
World were upset by that tremendous upheaval which
today is known as the American Revolution.

Chapter IV.

Thomas Jefferson, with a pair of scissors, a pot of paste, a bottle of ink, a goose-quill and a serene conscience, does a bit of editing and (greatly to his own surprise) gains for himself a ranking place among the immortals of history.

THE AMERICAN REVOLUTION seems to lie a very long time behind us. So many things have happened since then, especially during the last thirty years, that this glorious episode in our national history has somehow dwindled down to an event of very small proportions. What the contemporaries of General Washington called a "battle," we now dismiss as a minor skirmish, which indeed it was when we compare those conflicts of our Revolution to the gigantic encounters of millions of men which have taken place on the plains of Russia, and whenever we feel sorry for Washington and his soldiers at Valley Forge, a still small voice is apt to ask us, "But how about the people of Norway and Greece and Holland and all the other European countries who went through the third year of their Valley Forge, enduring their tortures and hardships not only in the winter but also during the summer, spring and fall?"

Also, we of the present generation have become so accustomed to such an endless variety of complicated "causes" and in so many parts of the world that we are somewhat baffled by a struggle in which both sides spoke the same language, obeyed the same laws, shared the same traditions and yet got so hopelessly on each other's nerves and into each other's hair (to use a picturesque if slightly vulgar expression) that finally they must shoot at each other with rifles and stab at each other with swords and pitchforks in order to reach some kind of a solution.

What, then, was the real cause for this family quarrel?

We know that this conflict (unlike most wars) was not the result of a rivalry for territory or for gold mines or oil wells or the supremacy of one race over another. It was something so new that few people were able to recognize it at the time and, indeed, even today there are historians who fail to see that, in the end, the English of the Old World were bound to fight the English of the New World because the English of the New World had ceased to be Englishmen and had become Americans.

Those who lived in the cities or close to the seaboard and who therefore were in constant communication with the folks at home found it comparatively easy to remain more or less British in their tastes and in their manner of living and their habits, and they would "M'Lord" a British official just as heartily as if they had never left the mother country. But an energetic and independent young fellow who had grown up in the wilderness and who, like the Jeffersons (both father and son), had never let anyone else do for him what he could do for himself—no, such a proud and independent young frontiersman was not going to take orders from an overbearing young whippersnapper who had been sent to America in an official capacity because his mother happened to be the niece of a duke or the sister of a bishop of England nobody had ever heard of. And if this American served in the local militia as a major and knew how to fight the wild Injuns, he felt little desire to obey a lieutenant in his majesty's regular army who treated a seasoned old colonial major (even if he happened to be a certain George Washington) as if he belonged to an inferior breed, forever excluded from the higher ranks.

We are all of us familiar with that list of grievances which is expected to explain the final outbreak of hostilities between the mother country and the colonies. But none of those so-called "wrongs"—no matter how eloquently they were exposed by our local politicians and orators—were really of sufficient importance to have been the cause of such a definite break. That the colonists were not represented in Parliament was true, but since the vast majority of all Englishmen in England itself were not enjoying any kind of direct representation, that was hardly a reason for going to war.

Or take the question of the taxes the mother country levied on the colonists, including the infamous tea tax, which, compared to what we casually pay our government today on everything we eat and drink, was less than nothing at all. Now we know that those colonial taxes, far from being an outrageous levy upon American incomes, were used to reimburse the mother country for at least part of the expenses which it had incurred in defending the colonies against the aggressions of the French and in protecting the northern frontier from further inroads by the armies of the French kings and their Indian allies.

Or, just to choose another item that is often mentioned, there was the matter of not being permitted to trade with other countries than the homeland. Every colonial nation insisted upon such a monopoly and the laws of France and Spain were infinitely more severe in this respect than those of England. Furthermore, these trade regulations were very carelessly enforced among the British colonies along the Atlantic seaboard and they were broken every day and night of the year.

Nowadays the world is very apt to rid itself of problems which it does not understand by saying that they are "psychological problems," which means that they have something to do with the human psyche or soul. That is perhaps too easy a way out of the difficulty, but in this instance the difference in the "souls," in the outlook upon life of the English at home and their colonial subjects abroad, had a great deal more to do with the explosion that followed than anything else of either a social or economic nature. After a century and a half of an entirely different kind of life, the Britishers and the Americans just did not happen to see most things from the same angle. Once such a point has been reached, nations are pretty sure to go to war with each other, no matter how hard they may have tried to come to an understanding and to patch up their differences by means of conferences and debates.

But before the first shot is actually fired, they will, of course, spend years jockeying for position, trying to present their own case in such a light that it will look to the rest of the world as if they, and only they, were in the right, and bolstering up their own good cause with arguments that are so plain and simple and so convincing that no one can possibly fail to be impressed. It was during this period, when England and the colonists bombarded each other with pamphlets and tracts and broadsheets, that Thomas Jefferson was discovered to have exceptional gifts as a literary advocate of the cause of the colonists.

In the year 1769 Thomas Jefferson had been chosen a member of the House of Burgesses. He went to every succeeding assembly until the year 1775, when he was elected as a representative to the Continental Congress that was held in Philadelphia in September of that year.

Thomas Jefferson was a very mediocre speaker but the colonies were already full of people who talked too much and much too often, and the Jeffersonian lack of a glib tongue was more than made up for by his ability to fish little words out of a tiny bottle of ink and then put them together in such a way that they made sense.

And now a slight indisposition gave Jefferson a chance to make full use of his writing talent, for when the moment had come to sum up the different grievances of the colonists and put them down, black on white, in a number of resolutions that were to be sent to London, it was the delegate from Albemarle County, enjoying a short period of enforced rest, who was deemed to be the logical man for this task.

In this way, Thomas Jefferson began his career as one of the most effective paper agitators for the cause of the Americans.

He started in the year 1775 with a pamphlet called *A Summary View of the Rights of America.* Nothing came of it, nor of the other barrels of printed wood pulp that were sent to England by every returning vessel. Finally the day came when the colonists felt that it was necessary to take some kind of decisive action and that, as an orderly and law-abiding people, they should inform not only England but the world at large why the Americans felt it their duty to rise in open rebellion against the mother country. For this purpose, no one seemed more fit than the distinguished delegate from Virginia, who had now come to Philadelphia, that there, with the representatives of the other thirteen colonies, he might decide upon the best course of action.

The first colony to step boldly forward with a list of grievances had been North Carolina, which as early as April of the year 1776 had authorized its delegate to the forthcoming Continental Congress to warn the others that some drastic action would soon become necessary. But North Carolina was only ready to go ahead if the other colonies felt the same way, a course for which we can hardly blame them, as a defeat of their plans would have meant execution of their leaders at the hands of a British hangman.

To Virginia fell the honor of having been the first colony which actually mentioned that ominous word, inde-

The Raleigh Tavern where, in the Apollo Room, Thomas Jefferson dined.

pendence. On the seventh of June of the year 1776, Richard Henry Lee of Virginia, acting on instructions given him a month earlier, laid down before the Continental Congress a resolution which read: "These united colonies are and of right ought to be free and independent states."

The very boldness of the suggestion must have caused great embarrassment among the vast majority of the people, not only of England but everywhere else, for the theory of government of that day (as accepted by practically everybody) recognized the bond between a king and his subjects as something sacred, and to arise against one's annointed ruler was considered almost as wicked as to revolt against the will of Almighty God.

It is true that once before—in the year 1649—the people of England had rid themselves of an unpopular sovereign by the rather drastic expedient of chopping off his head. And although few people knew about it (Thomas Jefferson was an exception), the inhabitants of the Netherlands, almost two centuries before, had done something very much like it. That had happened in July of the year 1581. Then, just as in the America of the year 1776, the people who had been obliged to take such a formidable step, who had seen themselves forced to break the sacred covenant between a ruler and his subjects, had felt the necessity of presenting to the world at large a long legal document which contained all the arguments upon which they based their contention that what they were doing was not merely according to the laws of Man but also to the dictates of God. "Since all government," so they had written "as it had been instituted by the Lord Himself, was identical with the relationship that existed between a shepherd and his flock, it became the duty of the flock to rid itself of that shepherd, once he had ceased to be their protector and had become their oppressor and had given evidence that no remonstrance on the part of his patient flock could persuade him to repent of his ways and treat his charges with reasonable kindness."

It is difficult for us to recapture the feeling that must have been in the hearts of the people of those days. We elect those who are supposed to rule over us. A few of them we know personally. Most of them are merely names we have read on some billboard. Some we respect, some we do not respect quite so much. But, good, bad or indifferent, we regard them as plain, ordinary fellow-citizens, and none of us thinks that Heaven has had anything to do with whether Bill Jones is elected congressman or not. And when we hear our father say that it will be an outrage if we allow that fellow who wants to become sheriff to get more than a dozen votes, we duly say, "Sure it will!" and promptly forget all about him.

Our attitude towards these officials who serve us is about the same as it is towards the man who sells us our groceries and who delivers our milk, except that as a rule the latter is a much more real person to us. We are the best of friends with him and deal with him not only because he gives us good service but because we like him sincerely and would hate to hurt his feelings by going to someone else. But if, for one reason or another, we should no longer be satisfied, then we would change, without any pangs of conscience, and we would go to some other store without the slightest remorse. We are apt to treat those who rule us—those whom we ourselves have elected to rule over us—in exactly the same way. As long as they give us satisfactory service, they are pretty sure of being allowed to hold onto their jobs. But the moment they no longer give such satisfaction, it is "Out with them!" and we look for somebody else to take their places.

But not so to the contemporaries of Thomas Jefferson nor to those who had defied tyranny before him. Trained under the age-old conceptions of loyalty and obedience to their rulers, they must first of all persuade themselves that they were right and that they could not possibly do otherwise, before they would ever consider such a far and deep-reaching step.

As I explained a moment ago, the line of defense which the Dutch predecessors of Jefferson followed had been based upon the argument that a king had been placed over his subjects even as a shepherd is placed over his sheep, to guard them and protect them and keep them from harm. If the king, therefore, instead of doing this, treated his subjects—his sheep—with cruelty and contempt and neglected them in every possible manner, then it became the good right of the sheep to go forth and look for another shepherd.

In our own Declaration of Independence, that line of reasoning is also closely followed. In order to gain the good will of the world at large, it was necessary to show that no other course had remained open to the poor sheep of Virginia and Massachusetts and New York and all the other colonies than the one they had finally taken. But exactly how this was to be accomplished and accomplished in such a way that no one could raise any kind of valïd objection, that was something else again and something no one in the convention could foretell. And so the convention did what similar large groups of men (or women) will always do when they are not quite sure of themselves—they appointed a committee.

This committee consisted of the venerable Benjamin Franklin, the "wise old man" of the convention; of John Adams, who represented the New England influence and who was to become our second president; of Thomas Jefferson, for the province of Virginia; of Roger Sherman from Connecticut, who afterwards became treasurer of Yale College; and of Thomas Livingstone, who is perhaps best remembered as the man who financed Robert Fulton when that distinguished painter began his experiments with his steamboat on the Hudson River.

As usually happens once a committee has been appointed, the members recognized that nothing of any importance would ever be accomplished if they allowed it to become a debating club, and that the best purposes would be served if they let the ablest members of their council provide them with a kind of outline or working-plan, whereupon the rest of them could discuss the pro's and con's until, in the end, they had something that would be satisfactory to all of them.

Many of the delegates to the convention felt that the resolution of Richard Henry Lee, that "these United Colonies are and of right ought to be free and independent States," was a marvelous starting point for their further decisions and actions. But the more conservative members still hesitated.

Please keep this fact well in mind—that most of the members belonged to a class of society which was running a grave personal risk in case there should be an open attempt at rebellion against His British Majesty's sovereign power, and should it fail, their fate would not be a happy one. For they were not at all like the farmers of Vermont or Virginia, who could safely hooray for independence without running a direct risk to their own lives. Suppose there was an outbreak of hostilities and suppose the King sent an army of hired Germans to reconquer the colonies? Then, it is true, the houses and barns of those rebellious farmers would be burned and their cattle would have their throats cut (as happened actually to Thomas Jefferson's cattle when Virginia was invaded by the English), but they themselves could quite easily escape into the woods and there, with their trusted axes, they soon would have built themselves new homes and their wives would have spun new garments for the children and their grandmothers would have dipped fresh candles into the grease-barrels and next spring they would have laid out a few patches of land on which to grow corn and cabbage, and after a short while they would have lived about as well or as badly as they had done before. They had always been on the fringe of poverty and it was only their self-reliance which had saved them, and their self-reliance was something they could take with them wherever they went.

But what of the rich merchants and shipowners and

moneylenders (they usually called themselves bankers) and real estate owners of New York and Philádelphia and Boston and Charleston? To them, if they had declared themselves in favor of total independence and if the King had been victorious, it would have meant the end of everything. They would have lost every piece of property they and their ancestors had accumulated during a century and a half of hard work. Their houses would have been occupied by the royal officers. Their silver plate (which they deeply loved as a symbol of their distinguished position in society) would have been packed off to England and would henceforth have graced the tables of their conquerors. Their horses would have been taken out of their comfortable stables to drag the royal artillery in pursuit of the rebels and their wives and daughters (accustomed to order their dresses from London and Paris) would have been obliged to hire out as domestic servants.

That was a pretty terrible prospect and one that could not fail to impress those who were now placed before so momentous a decision. An act of open defiance of the royal authority meant something very different to a Thomas Jefferson—a rich landowner with thousands of acres and a lovely house, full of beautiful furniture, and charming guests and good food and good wines—than to a Patrick Henry, whose home groaned under a burden of debt. It was one thing to John Adams, the patriot of Braintree, Massachusetts, who soon afterwards moved to Boston as offering a wider field for his legal and political abilities, and something else to a rough and ready fellow like Ethan Allen, the leader of the Green Mountain Boys from Vermont, who was much richer in his vocabulary than in the more tangible goods of this world.

We of today, when kings and emperors and presidents and all kinds of other potentates are dethroned and removed from office without the slightest ceremonial, sometimes feel that our great-great-grandfathers of the glorious Revolutionary era ought to have been much more eager about their efforts to achieve immediate independence. We realize that many of them hesitated and debated and wrangled for months at a time and passed endless resolutions and counter-resolutions before they finally declared that they wished to rid themselves, for once and for all, of their unpopular sovereign. But let us be fair to them. They had to make a decision which we ourselves will never have to make unless some indestructible dictator succeeds in coming over here and turns us into a subject race. And the very idea of such a catastrophe is enough to make most of us feel slightly ill.

But when in the middle of the month of June of the year 1776, Thomas Jefferson and his fellow-committee members sat themselves down to give fuller and more concrete expression to Richard Henry Lee's brief resolution about "complete independence," they and those who gave them instructions to do so committed an act of the greatest possible courage, for they let their convictions and their consciences guide them towards a step which, if it had failed to be successful, would have meant the death and ruin of all of them.

The committee of five duly came together and decided

The Patriots met in quiet places.

that Thomas Jefferson, as being by far the cleverest interpreter of their ideas, should draw up some kind of a document which would inform not only His Majesty, the
King of England, and his ministers, but also the world at
large, of what the colonists intended to do and which
would explain the reasons which compelled them to take

so far-reaching a step.

Upon his arrival in Philadelphia, Thomas Jefferson had taken rooms in the house of a German bricklayer by the name of Graaf or Graf. Jefferson occupied the whole of the second floor, but it must have been a small house, as his quarters consisted only of a parlor and bedroom. It was (as far as he himself could remember afterwards, but he often forgot such items on purpose) situated on the south side of Market Street, between Seventh and Eighth Streets, in case you are interested in such details. He composed his first rough drafts on a writing box, made according to his own specifications by one Benjamin Randall, a Philadelphia cabinetmaker.

Did the whole of that ever-famous preamble to the Declaration of Independence now suddenly flow out of Thomas Jefferson's pen as the waters gushed out of the rock struck by the staff of Moses? It did not, and until the end of his days he was forever insisting that there was nothing supernatural about his declaration but that, on the contrary, it had been a piece of judicious "editing" of quite a number of ideas and opinions, which had long since been freely circulated among the hundreds of pamphleteers who were writing either in favor of independence or against it.

How could it have been otherwise, since pamphlets discussing "the situation" had been pouring from the presses of both countries for at least a dozen years and were as common as booklets on "How to Win Lasting Peace" and "The Brave New World" are at the moment I am writing this. Indeed, it looked as if the whole nation had gone writing-mad and it therefore had become exceedingly difficult not to use expressions which others had already used before.

John Adams, Jefferson's rival from Massachusetts, an able and patriotic citizen but a man who lacked all the charm and big-heartedness that were so characteristic of his Virginia colleague, came forward with the accusation that all this fuss about the glorious Declaration of Independence was so much poppycock; that all of the ideas it contained had been part of every orator's stock in trade for years; that whole passages of it had been lifted bodily out of a pamphlet by James Otis (a pamphlet, by the way, which Thomas Jefferson had never read); that John Locke, the most popular of the English philosophers of the seventeenth century, had already discussed most of these political theories about the duties of sovereigns towards their subjects which were to be found in our Declaration of Independence; and quite a lot more—all of the same nature.

But what did this prove? It proved nothing at all. For if John Adams had wanted to go back still a few thousand years more to prove that Thomas Jefferson had not been the originator of the wisdom contained in his Declaration of Independence, he could have done so very conveniently by quoting the main passages from the Sermon on the Mount. But those selfsame words of Jesus about the brotherhood of man and the necessity of all of God's creatures living with each other in the fullest enjoyment of the fruits of their labors, now for the first time found themselves expressed, not in a religious exhortation but in a practical document of state.

And that, I think, is the reason why the world will remember the name of Thomas Jefferson long after most of his fellow-laborers in the holy cause of our national independence shall have been forgotten. For Thomas Jefferson was much more than a statesman who belonged to one single country or group of people. By his Declaration of Independence he made himself the prophet and spokesman of all those true benefactors of mankind who ever since the beginning of time and in every part of the globe have given their heart's blood to assure their fellowmen, not only of life and liberty, but also of a fair chance to achieve that modicum of personal happiness which should be the birthright of every animated being, created after the image of God Almighty.

On July second of the year 1776, the Continental Congress voted in favor of independence. Two days later, on a hot and sultry fourth of July, it accepted (with a few small and unimportant changes) the formal Declaration of Independence of the United States of America, as it had been composed by the chairman of the committee of five which had been entrusted with the task of presenting the case of the exasperated colonists to the judgment of the world at large.

From a formal historical point of view, we could therefore claim that our country is two days older than it actually is. But when this momentous resolution was read to the soldiers of the Republic it was dated, "In Congress, July 4th, 1776. A Declaration by the respresentatives of the United States of America in General Congress assem-

July 4, 1776. In the beginning was the idea.

bled." And what was good enough for those brave men who gave us our freedom is good enough for us.

The original Declaration of Independence, by the way, had a very curious existence. During the first hundred and one years after it had been penned in Mr. Graf's humble parlor, it enjoyed no permanent place of residence. It was considered a public curiosity and was forever on the move. It traveled from one state to the next and resided temporarily in at least ten different cities. Twice, first during the war of the Revolution and for a second time during the burning and plundering of the city of Washington by the British in the year 1812, it was almost captured by the enemy. After a century of such dangerous wanderings, the ink had been exposed to so much light that the writing had begun to grow very faint and the signatures, from the constant rolling of the parchment, had begun to crack and would soon have become entirely undecipherable. It was then decided to send it for safe keeping to the Department of State. But that old edifice, should it ever have caught fire, would have burned like a haystack, and so finally, in the year 1921, it was removed to a specially constructed safe in the Library of Congress. Even there, should Washington ever be bombed, it might come to grief and therefore I would like to make a suggestion.

Here is that famous document as it was originally reported to the Continental Congress by Thomas Jefferson himself. I have borrowed it from Bernard Mayo's most excellent book entitled *Jefferson Himself*, and I hope he will forgive me for this act of trespass if here and now I urge all of you to get hold of this rarely entertaining and instructive volume and read it for yourselves, as then and only then will you come to know Thomas Jefferson as he really was.

The parts of the document that were struck out by Congress during its debates have been placed in brackets. Those parts which Congress inserted are printed in italics. Do you know what the suggestion is I would like to make? It is this: that you learn all of those few pages to follow by heart. That, of course, is quite a job but it can be done, or at least you can memorize enough of it to know the main points. And once you have done that, you will be ever conscious of your duties as a good American, a good democrat and therefore a faithful servant of your fellowmen.

A DECLARATION BY THE REPRESENTATIVES OF THE UNITED STATES OF AMERICA, IN (GENERAL) CONGRESS ASSEMBLED.

When in the course of human events it becomes necessary for one people to dissolve the political bands which have connected them with one another, and to assume among the powers of the earth the separate and equal station to which the laws of nature and of nature's God entitle them, a decent respect to the opinions of mankind requires that they should declare the causes which impel them to the separation.

We hold these truths to be self-evident: that all men

are created equal; that they are endowed by their Creator with (inherent and) *certain* inalienable rights; that among these are life, liberty, and the pursuit of happiness; that to secure these rights, governments are instituted among men, deriving their just powers from the consent of the governed; that whenever any form of government becomes destructive of these ends, it is the right of the people to alter or to abolish it, and to institute new government, laying its foundation on such principles, and organizing its powers in such form, as to them shall seem most likely to effect their safety and happiness. Prudence, indeed, will dictate that governments long established should not be changed for light and transient causes; and accordingly all experience hath shown that mankind are more disposed to suffer while evils are sufferable, than to right themselves by abolishing the forms to which they are accustomed. But when a long train of abuses and usurpations, (begun at a distinguished period and) pursuing invariably the same object, evinces a design to reduce them under absolute despotism, it is their right, it is their duty to throw off such government, and to provide new guards for their future security. Such has been the patient sufferance of these colonies; and such is now the necessity which constrains them to (expunge) *alter* their former systems of government. The history of the present King of Great Britain is a history of (unremitting) *repeated* injuries and usurpations, (among which appears no solitary fact to contradict the uniform tenor of the rest, but all have) *all having* in direct object the establishment of an absolute tyranny over these States. To prove this, let facts be submitted to a candid world (for the truth of which we pledge a faith yet unsullied by falsehood).

He has refused his assent to laws the most wholesome and necessary for the public good.

He has forbidden his governors to pass laws of immediate and pressing importance, unless suspended in their operation till his assent should be obtained; and, when so suspended, he has utterly neglected to attend to them.

He has refused to pass other laws for the accommodation of large districts of people unless those people would relinquish the right of representation in the legislature, a right inestimable to them, and formidable to tyrants only.

He has called together legislative bodies at places unusual, uncomfortable, and distant from the depository of their public records, for the sole purpose of fatiguing them into compliance with his measures.

He has dissolved representative houses repeatedly (and continually) for opposing with manly firmness his invasions on the rights of the people.

He has refused for a long time after such dissolutions to cause others to be elected, whereby the legislative powers, incapable of annihilation, have returned to the people at large for their exercise, the state remaining, in the meantime, exposed to all the dangers of invasion from without and convulsions within.

He has endeavored to prevent the population of these states; for that purpose obstructing the laws for naturalization of foreigners, refusing to pass others to encourage their migrations hither, and raising the conditions of new appropriations of lands.

He has (suffered) *obstructed* the administration of justice (totally to cease in some of these states) *by* refusing his assent to laws for establishing judiciary powers.

He has made (our) judges dependent on his will alone for the tenure of their offices, and the amount and payment of their salaries.

He has erected a multitude of new offices, (by a self-assumed power) and sent hither swarms of new officers to harass our people and eat out their substance.

He has kept among us in times of peace standing armies (and ships of war) without the consent of our legislatures.

He has affected to render the military independent of, and superior to, the civil power.

He has combined with others to subject us to a jurisdiction foreign to our constitutions and unacknowledged by our laws, giving his assent to their acts of pretended legislation for quartering large bodies of armed troops among us; for protecting them by a mock trial from punishment for any murders which they should commit on the inhabitants of these states; for cutting off our trade with all parts of the world; for imposing taxes on us without our consent; for depriving us *in many cases* of the benefits of trial by jury; for transporting us beyond seas to be tried for pretended offences; for abolishing the free system of English laws in a neighboring province, establishing therein an arbitrary government, and enlarging its boundaries, so as to render it at once an example and fit instrument for introducing the same absolute rule into these (states) *colonies;* for taking away our charters, abolishing our most valuable laws, and altering fundamentally the forms of our governments; for suspending our own legislatures, and declaring themselves invested with power to legislate for us in all cases whatsoever.

He has abdicated government here (withdrawing his governors, and declaring us out of his allegiance and protection) *by declaring us out of his protection, and waging war against us.*

He has plundered our seas, ravaged our coasts, burnt our towns, and destroyed the lives of our people.

He is at this time transporting large armies of foreign mercenaries to complete the works of death, desolation, and tyranny already begun with circumstances of cruelty and perfidy *scarcely paralleled in the most barbarous ages, and totally* unworthy the head of a civilized nation.

He has constrained our fellow citizens taken captive on the high seas to bear arms against their country, to become the executioners of their friends and brethren, or to fall themselves by their hands.

He has *excited domestic insurrection among us, and has* endeavored to bring on the inhabitants of our frontiers, the merciless Indian savages, whose known rule of warfare is an undistinguished destruction of all ages, sexes, and conditions (of existence).

(He has incited treasonable insurrections of our fellow citizens, with the allurements of forefeiture and confiscation of our property.

(He has waged cruel war against human nature itself,

violating its most sacred rights of life and liberty in the persons of a distant people who never offended him, captivating and carrying them into slavery in another hemisphere, or to incur miserable death in their transportation thither. This piratical warfare, the opprobrium of INFIDEL. powers, is the warfare of the CHRISTIAN king of Great Britain. Determined to keep open a market where MEN should be bought and sold, he has prostituted his negative for suppressing every legislative attempt to prohibit or to restrain this execrable commerce. And that this assemblage of horrors might want no fact of distinguished die, he is now exciting those very people to rise in arms among us, and to purchase that liberty of which he has deprived them, by murdering the people on whom he also obtruded them: thus paying off former crimes committed against the LIBERTIES of one people, with crimes which he urges them to commit against the LIVES of another.)

In every stage of these oppressions we have petitioned for redress in the most humble terms: our repeated petitions have been answered only by repeated injuries.

A prince whose character is thus marked by every act which may define a tyrant is unfit to be the ruler of a *free* people (who mean to be free. Future ages will scarcely believe that the hardiness of one man adventured, within the short compass of twelve years only, to lay a foundation so broad and so undisguised for tyranny over a people fostered and fixed in principles of freedom.)

Nor have we been wanting in attentions to our British brethren. We have warned them from time to time of at-

They remained steadfast during the four years of hunger, want, neglect and treason.

tempts by their legislature to extend (a) *an unwarrantable* jurisdiction over (these our states) *us.* We have reminded them of the circumstances of our emigration and settlement here, (no one of which could warrant so strange a pretension; that these were effected at the expense of our own blood and treasure, unassisted by the wealth or the strength of Great Britain; that in constituting indeed our several forms of government, we had adopted one common king, thereby laying a foundation for perpetual league and amity with them; but that submission to their parliament was no part of our constitution, nor ever in idea, if history may be credited: and,) we *have* appealed to their native justice and magnanimity (as well as to) *and we have conjured them by* the ties of our common kindred to disavow these usurpations which (were likely to) *would inevitably* interrupt our connection and correspondence. They too have been deaf to the voice of justice and of consanguinity, (and when occasions have been given them, by the regular course of their laws, of removing from their councils the disturbers of our harmony, they have, by their free election, re-established them in power. At this very time too, they are permitting their chief magistrate to send over not only soldiers of our common blood, but Scotch and foreign mercenaries to invade and destroy us. These facts have given the last stab to agonizing affection, and manly spirit bids us to renounce forever these unfeeling brethren. We must endeavor to forget our former love for them, and hold them as we hold the rest of mankind, enemies in war, in peace friends. We might have been a free and a great people together; but a communication of grandeur and of freedom, it seems, is below their dignity. Be it so, since they will have it. The road to happiness and to glory is open to us, too. We will tread it apart from them, and) *we must therefore* acquiesce in the necessity which denounces our (eternal) separation *and hold* them as we hold the rest of mankind, enemies in war, in peace friends!

We, therefore, the representatives of the United States of America in General Congress assembled, *appealing to the supreme judge of the world for the rectitude of our intentions,* do in the name, and by the authority of the good people of these (states reject and renounce all allegiance and subjection to the kings of Great Britain and all others who may hereafter claim by, through or under them; we utterly dissolve all political connection which may heretofore have subsisted between us and the people or parliament of Great Britain: and finally we do assert and declare these colonies to be free and independent states,) *colonies, solemnly publish and declare, that these united colonies are, and of right ought to be, free and independent states; that they are absolved from all allegiance to the British crown, and that all political connection between them and the state of Great Britain is, and ought to be, totally dissolved;* and that as free and independent states they have full power to levy war, conclude peace, contract alliances, establish commerce, and to do all other acts and things which independent states may of right do.

And for the support of this declaration, *with a firm reliance on the protection of divine providence,* we mutually pledge to each other our lives, our fortunes, and our sacred honor.

Chapter V.

The last fifty years of a most useful life.

THOMAS JEFFERSON lived half a century after he had written his Declaration of Independence. During these fifty years, he did a stupendous amount of work, enough to have provided a dozen ordinary people with official careers that would have become the pride of their descendants.

After he had played his rôle in the Continental Congress of the year 1776, he went back to his native state in the hope of making it an example to the other twelve colonies. He wanted to put it on a truly democratic basis and he started by agitating for the abolishment of primogeniture and entail. Both of these words are of medieval origin and both of them go back to the Feudal Ages, when land was practically the only form of wealth and when every family tried to get hold of as much land as possible and then, by means of the law, tie it up in such a way that no matter what happened, the bulk of an estate was sure to descend from the father to his oldest son, without any of it being given to the other children.

Thomas Jefferson did not want to see the New World repeat all the mistakes of the old one and did his best to prevent the continuation of the feudal system on our side of the ocean. He had always maintained that the whole of the world belonged to the human race. He was not foolish enough to believe in the mental equality of all men. Far from it. Like Plato, two thousand years before, he felt that it was the duty of the state to give all the people an equal chance at education, so that it could be shown who were the dull-witted, the merely bright ones and the very bright ones, and then, so he hoped (for he was very much of an optimist), the very bright ones would consider it their privilege to serve the state and their less fortunate neighbors.

But neither did he have any great sympathy for the old and popular idea (popular especially among the richer classes) that a few children, by merely taking the trouble to be born, should therefore and for the rest of their days enjoy all the comforts and pleasures of this life. He believed in letting people work for everything they received, and because this was almost a holy conviction with him he did his best to break up a system that encouraged the exact opposite. Needless to say, this agitation for a more even distribution of the good things of this world did not increase his popularity among his well-to-do neighbors and it was not until the year 1785 that "entail" and "primogeniture" were abolished in Virginia.

Next he tackled the even more ticklish problem of religious liberty and introduced a bill for complete religious freedom in the state of Virginia. This bill, and then in a modified form, was not adopted until the year 1786, but Jefferson always considered it one of the most useful things he had done and asked that it be specially mentioned on the stone that was to cover his grave. He did not insist that that stone should also record the fact that he had been President of the United States. That, to him, was merely a detail of his career, like having been a justice of the peace. But his Declaration of Independence and his labors on behalf of religious freedom should be used as the main arguments which, so he hoped, entitled him to the respect and gratitude of his fellow-citizens.

And then there was a third item that would have to go on the obelisk that was to be erected over his final resting place. That third item was his fathership of the University of Virginia. He was very proud of having devoted so much of his energies to the cause of public education, of having fought so bravely for free public schools, for free public libraries, and for colleges and universities that should be absolutely free in their honest efforts to unravel at least a few of Nature's puzzles and to reveal a few of Nature's secrets, so that man should no longer be an absolute slave to his environment and should be able to dominate those forces which from the beginning of time had been a menace to his safety and should thereby increase his dignity as a creature created after the Lord's own image.

This Virginian philosopher and supreme literary craftsman was at heart a very practical person. That is why he gave us the decimal system in monetary matters and set us free from the hopelessly complicated duodecimal system of the mother country. I wish he had succeeded in doing the same thing for our weights and measures, so that today we would not be so completely out of step with the rest of the world. But it is too late now and nothing, I fear me, can be done about it.

He took great delight in keeping himself busy with such problems, for he could work on them while remaining peacefully at home, superintending and improving his own soil, experimenting with a variety of new foods, so that the average man might be able to support himself for less money and yet get better food values and raise a healthier family than he had ever done before.

In this respect, of course, he got nowhere at all. His beloved "average man" (whom he only came to understand a little better as he grew older), was as obstinate as a mule when it came to any drastic innovations in his own daily existence. He fought the new and healthy cereals and vegetables and fruits, with which Mr. Jefferson tried to make him happy, with obstinate unwillingness. He refused to let himself be convinced and stuck tenaciously to his frying-pan and to the mushy stuff which made him lose half of his family through the wrong kind of nutrition. But Jefferson, as I have pointed out all through these pages, was a true philosopher and he understood that the only way in which one can hope to love humanity is to learn to love it in spite of itself.

As for offices of state, these he accepted as a public duty when they came his way, but he never went after them, for they were not very much to his taste. They forced him to waste a great deal of valuable time on committee meetings and obliged him to live away from home, in New York and Philadelphia, the two cities which were the temporary capitals of our nation until the new capital in Virginia (on a site along the banks of the Potomac and not far away from General Washington's residence at Mount Vernon) should be ready for occupancy. But duty was duty and, having assisted at the birth of this new nation, he felt that he should at least remain faithful to it until it had outgrown the swaddling clothes and had learned to walk by itself. And so, when Dr. Benjamin Franklin, then in his seventy-eighth year, expressed the not unreasonable desire to be recalled from his post as American Ambassador to the Court of Versailles, it was Thomas Jefferson who succeeded him, though he was very careful to explain to the French Minister of Foreign Affairs that he did not "replace him," as no one could hope to replace the beaver-capped sage from Boston, Philadelphia and the world at large.

Thomas Jefferson remained five years in France and left just before the outbreak of the great revolution there. He had realized all along that the old French monarchy was doomed. Too few people had too much power and wealth, and by far too many had nothing at all. That was the prime fear which was the driving force in everything Jefferson tried to do as a leader of men. The New World (he repeated this assertion time and again) must never repeat the mistakes of the old one. It must give every man a fair chance. It must give every man a little bit of soil he could call his own and then he would be interested in that bit of soil and would work for it and fight for it and even die for it. And in the end, all these tiny little bits of soil would make up a large nation and every citizen would cherish that nation and its liberties as the highest of his possessions.

Jefferson, although he was not blind to the glaring
faults of the French people, came to like them for their
equally glaring virtues and he remained their steadfast
friend in spite of the inexcusable cruelties they committed during their revolution. His sympathy for the English, on the other hand, diminished rather than increased.
He had never forgiven them for the completely unneces-
sary acts of destruction and pillage of which they had
been guilty during their invasion of Virginia, but now he
had a chance to study them at home.

He was sent to London to negotiate a trade treaty between the United States and the former mother country.
In London he was received with studied rudeness and he
was made to feel as if he had been a runaway servant, instead of being the official representative of an independent and sovereign nation.

Shortly after his return to the United States, our people became divided into two groups which bitterly opposed each other. The Democratic elements were in
favor of the French Revolution and, though horrified by
a great many things that happened along the banks of
the Seine, they highly approved of the abolishment of a
royal form of government and the establishment of a republic, and they felt that of all nations, the republic of
the United States of America should be on the side of the
first European republic to be erected on the ruins of a
former tyranny.

The conservative elements, on the other hand, the
bankers and shipowners and real estate dealers and

money lenders of the big cities, headed by Alexander Hamilton (an immigrant from the West Indies and by birth far removed from any such aristocratic tendencies), were terribly afraid that a triumphant new democracy might strengthen the influence of our own popular form of government (much too popular to their tastes), and they almost forced our country into a war with France.

Jefferson stood aghast when he discovered how far a great many of the people of the United States had swung toward the conservative side during the five years of his absence. Having been appointed Secretary of State by President Washington, he did his best to make the ship of state sail a safe course between the extreme right and the extreme left, but from then on he knew that he would have to make a fight of it if he hoped to save the Republic from returning to a more or less monarchical form of government, for something like that was undoubtedly in the minds of Alexander Hamilton and his followers.

In the year 1793 Jefferson felt that he could no longer give his full loyalty to President Washington, who was much more under the influence of the aristocratic ideas of Hamilton than the democratic ones of his old neighbor, Mr. Thomas Jefferson of Albemarle County, Virginia. It was during this period that the followers of Thomas Jefferson grouped themselves together in a party which they called the Republican party and which was to become the starting point of what today we call the Democratic party.

In the year 1796, the Republicans succeeded in having Jefferson elected to the vice-presidency of the United

States and in the year 1801 he became the third President of the United States.

It was during his presidency that we acquired a great deal of additional territory through the purchase from France of Louisiana. With his support, Lewis and Clark undertook that famous voyage which opened the eyes of their contemporaries to the unlimited space (and practically empty space, too) which lay between them and the shores of the Pacific.

But here I could easily lose myself in endless details which really have very little to do with the Thomas Jefferson I wanted you to know, to understand and to love. It was Thomas Jefferson's misfortune to have to preside over our country while a terrific global war was raging all over our planet. And no matter what he did, he was sure to be denounced by either one side or the other and his motives were bound to be misunderstood and misrepresented by the leaders of those elements to whose advantage it was to oppose him.

So when in the year 1809, at the age of sixty-six, he definitely bade farewell to official life, packed up his papers, climbed on board his horse and returned to his beloved home on top of the Little Hill, it must have been one of the happiest days of his entire existence. From then on, he had only one ambition—the founding of the University of Virginia, an institution which he hoped to make the shining example of what a true seat of learning should be in a truly democratic nation and which should prove a shining example to all the other states.

And now a few words about the last years of this very

great man, who during that period fell a victim to his own generous impulses. Thomas Jefferson had been a true Virginia gentleman in the hospitality which he had extended not only to his own friends but to any curious stranger who came trotting up to his house to pay his respects to the famous sage of Monticello or (as was more likely) to satisfy his curiosity as to what the old gentleman looked like and whether it was really true that anybody who expressed a desire to stay for dinner would be provided with a free meal.

Alas, it was only too true. These hungry and thirsty pilgrims were not only entertained most liberally at the master's table but if they showed the slightest inclination to tarry, they were provided with a bed for a week or a month or even a couple of months. In the end, this pack of hungry wolves actually ate poor Thomas Jefferson out of house and home. For though he did not know it, he had grown too old to be able to manage so vast an estate all alone, but he had no sons and no near male relatives who could relieve him of at least a few of his duties. And then he had done something that is always very dangerous and that may lead even the most careful of business men into trouble. He had endorsed the note of a good friend. The good friend went bankrupt. It was Thomas Jefferson who had to make up the difference. It was a considerable sum and it ruined him.

Indeed, the situation in which he thereupon found himself was so serious that for quite a long time it looked as if he would actually lose his beloved Monticello— that it would have to be surrendered to his creditors.

Jefferson climbed on board his horse and returned to his beloved home on top of the Little Hill.

When news of this impending disaster began to be murmured around, let it be said to the everlasting honor of at least part of his contemporaries that they at once took steps to prevent what would have been nothing short of a national disgrace.

Just before Jefferson (as a last desperate measure) was going to ask permission of the authorities in Williamsburg to sell his estates by means of a lottery, his friends in every part of the Union rallied to his assistance. From all over the country, small and large sums of money began to find their way to Monticello. But in the end, these voluntary contributions netted only $16,000, and after almost half a century in the service of the Republic, Thomas Jefferson found himself $20,000 in debt. This relief, therefore, was only of a temporary nature, and as soon as Thomas Jefferson was dead his creditors once more marched forward and the old gentleman's daughter was forced to sell her father's estate to the highest bidder.

The burial plot was not included in the sale. It remained the property of the descendants of the man who had given us our Declaration of Independence. A small obelisk which mentioned the few deeds by which this departed prophet wished to be remembered by his descendants was gradually smashed to bits by curious visitors who were eager for souvenirs, and eventually every trace of his happy existence among the mountains of Virginia might have disappeared if it had not been for an act of true charity on the part of a retired naval officer, one Uriah P. Levy, who, having got title to the Monticello estate, restored it as carefully as possible to what it had looked like during the days when Thomas Jefferson himself had lived there.

Just before the first World War, a movement was started to acquire Monticello for the nation. The descendants of the original purchasers (who had been most generous in letting everyone visit their property) thereupon surrendered Monticello to the Thomas Jefferson Memorial Association and in the year 1923 Monticello became what it should always have been and must remain forever—a shrine where all the people of the United States may revere the memory of one of the greatest of their own nation.

And now you are, I suppose, still curious to know exactly how this most useful and patriotic citizen died, whether in his last moments he left a message to the nation he had helped found. No, he did not. Such a thing would have smacked of the dramatic, and Jefferson did not care for dramatics. Absolute simplicity of thought and action had always been one of his main characteristics and he left this world as quietly and as unobtrusively as he had entered it.

After his University of Virginia had opened its doors, he withdrew from life more and more. Another fall from his horse, as a result of which he broke a wrist, seriously interfered with one of this few remaining pleasures, that of corresponding with his friends. But he derived great satisfaction from a visit of his old Revolutionary comrade, the famous French general, Lafayette, who made his appearance at Monticello in the year 1825 and spent several happy days there, sitting quietly in the sun and renewing memories of the olden times, when his host had been Governor of Virginia and he, the Frenchman, had been fighting the British army among those selfsame hills upon which they now gazed from the peaceful top of Mr. Jefferson's final retreat.

Early in June of the year 1826, Thomas Jefferson's friends noticed that he was beginning to give alarming signs of physical exhaustion and that his mind would occasionally wander away from the subject at hand. Jefferson was fully aware of his situation.

"I am like an old watch," he told a visitor who tried to assure him that soon he would be his old self again. "I am like a very old watch. Here a pinion is worn out and there a wheel no longer will give service, and I am afraid it can't go on much longer."

Then came the fourth of July of the year 1826 and half a century had gone by since the ringing of the bells had first announced the birth of that new nation which was to become known as the United States of America. Once again the bells were ringing, but when they ceased to proclaim their cheerful message of liberty and hope, Thomas Jefferson had passed on to his final reward. And he was standing before that altar of God upon which, at the beginning of his career, he had sworn eternal hostility against every form of tyranny over the mind of man.

Servant of Humanity, well done! Well hast thou fought
The better fight, who singly hast maintained
Against a ruthless tyranny the cause
Of Freedom and of Truth.

Afterthought.

UP TO THIS POINT, you have only heard what the author of this book had to say about Thomas Jefferson. But before we bid each other farewell, I think that it would serve a good purpose if I gave you a change to hear Mr. Jefferson speak for himself and, if the publishers will give me just a few pages more, I shall reprint one or two of Thomas Jefferson's own letters and then you will understand why it was such a pleasure for me to make his acquaintance.

If, for example, I had got hold of that little discourse of his upon "the uselessness of arguing," I would have been a much happier man (and probably much pleasanter, too) than I now have been, for I would not have spent quite so much time upon useless disputes which got none of us anywhere and merely wasted valuable hours which we could have spent much better playing with the grandchildren or taking Mungo out for a walk.

AN ESSAY ON GOOD HUMOR

I shall be sending on to Philadelphia a grandson of about fifteen years of age. . . . Without that bright fancy which captivates, I am in hopes he possesses sound judgment and much observation, and, what I value more than all things, good humor. For thus I estimate the qualities of the mind: 1, good humor; 2, integrity; 3, industry; 4, science. The preference of the first to the second quality may not at first be acquiesced in; but certainly we had all rather associate with a good-humored, light-principled man than with an ill-tempered rigorist in morality.

I have mentioned good humor as one of the preservatives of our peace and tranquillity. It is among the most effectual, and its effect is so well imitated and aided, artificially, by politeness, that this also becomes an acquisition of first-rate value. In truth, politeness is artificial good humor, it covers the natural want of it, and ends by rendering habitual a substitute nearly equivalent to the real virtue. It is the practice of sacrificing to those whom we meet in society all the little conveniences and preferences which will gratify them and deprive us of nothing worth a moment's consideration; it is the giving a pleasing and flattering turn to our expressions which will conciliate others and make them pleased with us as well as themselves. How cheap a price for the good will of another! When this is in return for a rude thing said by another, it brings him to his senses, it mortifies and corrects him in the most salutary way, and places him at the feet of your good nature, in the eyes of the company.

But in stating prudential rules for our government in society, I must not omit the important one of never entering into dispute or arguments with another. I never saw an instance of one or two disputants convincing the other by argument. I have seen many, on their getting warm, becoming rude and shooting one another. Conviction is the effect of our own dispassionate reasoning, either in soli-

tude, or weighing within ourselves, dispassionately, what we hear from others, standing uncommitted in argument ourselves. It was one of the rules which, above all others, made Doctor Franklin the most amiable of men in society, "Never to contradict anybody." If he was urged to announce an opinion, he did it rather by asking questions, as if for information, or by suggesting doubts.

When I hear another express an opinion which is not mine, I say to myself, he has a right to his opinion, as I to mine; why should I question it? His error does me no injury, and shall I become a Don Quixote, to bring all men by force of argument to one opinion? If a fact be misstated, it is probably he is gratified by a belief of it, and I have no right to deprive him of the gratification. . . .

As I see it there are two classes of disputants most frequently to be met with among us. The first is of young students, just entered the threshold of science, with a first view of its outlines not yet filled up with the details and modifications which a further progress would bring to their knowledge. The other consists of the ill-tempered and rude men in society who have taken up a passion for politics. . . .

You will be more exposed than others to have these animals shaking their horns at you, because of the relation in which you stand with me. Full of political venom, and willing to see me and to hate me as a chief in the antagonist party, your presence will be to them what the vomit grass is to the sick dog, a nostrum for producing ejaculation. Look upon them exactly with that eye, and pity them as objects to whom you can administer only occasional ease. My character is not within their power. It is in the

*hands of my fellow-citizens at large, and will be consigned
to honor or infamy by the verdict of the republican mass
of our country, according to what themselves will have
seen, not what their enemies and mine shall have said.*

And here is another subject upon which I would like to
quote Thomas Jefferson, for the moment one lets it be
known that, in one's own opinion, the world will never
rise superior to its leaders and that good leadership,
therefore, is half of the battle of life, someone is sure to
get up and ask you, with a deep frown on his brow and
an accusing finger pointed straight at you, "And what, my
dear sir, about Thomas Jefferson and his belief in man's
equality? That is the basis of our democratic philosophy
of life, this belief that all men are born equal, and did he
not put that point ahead of all others—that all men are
born equal?"

Thomas Jefferson indeed incorporated these words into
the preamble to his Declaration of Independence, but
Thomas Jefferson was a very wise gentleman. He never
tried to be brighter than the good Lord Himself and since
the good Lord has been pleased to give us a universe in
which no two items (mountains, oceans, sparrows, ele-
phants or microbes) are absolutely equal, Thomas Jefferson was undoubtedly thinking of "equality before the
law" rather than "equality of brain or brawn" when he
wrote that sentence into the first part of his ever-famous
document of state.

To bear me out upon this point, I shall now reprint part
of a letter which he addressed to his predecessor in the

Presidency, John Adams, and which he wrote in the year 1812. The subject under discussion is that of "A true aristocracy," and here is the letter.

I agree with you, my good friend, that there is a natural aristocracy among men. The grounds of this are virtue and talents. Formerly, bodily powers gave place among the aristoi. But since the invention of gunpowder has armed the weak as well as the strong with missile death, bodily strength, like beauty, good humor, politeness, and other accomplishments, has become but an auxiliary ground of distinction. There is also an artificial aristocracy founded on wealth and birth, without either virtue or talents, for with these it would belong to the first class. The natural aristocracy I consider as the most precious gift of nature for the instruction, the trusts, and government of society. And indeed it would have been inconsistent in creation to have formed man for the social state and not to have provided virtue and wisdom enough to manage the concerns of the society. May we not even say that that form of government is the best which provides the most effectually for a pure selection of these natural aristoi into the offices of government? The artificial aristocracy is a mischievous ingredient in government, and provision should be made to prevent its ascendancy.

On the question what is the best provision, you and I differ; but we differ as rational friends. . . . You think it best to put the pseudo-aristoi into a separate chamber of legislation, where they may be hindered from doing mischief by their coordinate branches, and where, also, they may be a protection to wealth against the agrarian and plundering enterprises of the majority of the people. I think that to give them power in order to prevent them from doing mischief is arming them for it, and increasing instead of remedying the evil. . . . I think the best remedy is exactly that provided by all our constitutions, to leave to the citizens the free election and separation of the aristoi from the pseudo-aristoi, of the wheat from the chaff. . . .

It is probable that our difference of opinion may in some measure be produced by a difference in character in those among whom we live. . . . There seems to be (in Massachusetts and Connecticut) a traditionary reverence for certain families which has rendered the officers of the government nearly hereditary. . . . But although this . . . may in some degree be founded in real family merit, yet in a much higher degree it has proceeded from your strict alliance of Church and State. These families are canonized in the eyes of the people on common principles, "You tickle me, and I will tickle you."

In Virginia we have nothing of this. . . . Laws drawn by myself laid the axe to the root of pseudo-aristocracy. And had another which I had prepared been adopted . . . our work would have been complete. It was a bill for the most general diffusion of learning. . . . Worth and genius would thus have been sought out from every condition of life, and completely prepared by education for defeating the competition of wealth and birth for public trusts. . . . I have great hope that some patriotic spirit will . . . call it up and make it the keystone of the arch of our government.

And here, finally, are a few of Thomas Jefferson's ideas upon the very important subject of education. Though they were written more than a century ago, they are so absolutely modern that they should be of interest to you, for the problem is still with us because, no matter what happens, the younger generation is still with us and it is always a problem and always has been and always will be, because no "older generation" would ever be happy if it did not have the younger generation to worry about.

I HAVE INDEED TWO GREAT MEASURES AT HEART

A part of my occupation, and by no means the least pleasing, is the direction of the studies of such young men as ask it. They place themselves in the neighboring village, and have the use of my library and counsel, and make a part of my society. . . . I endeavor to keep their attention fixed on the main objects of all science, the freedom and happiness of man. So that coming to bear a share in the councils and government of their country, they will keep ever in view the sole objects of all legitimate government.

I have indeed two great measures at heart, without which no republic can maintain itself in strength. 1. That of general education, to enable every man to judge for himself what will secure or endanger his freedom. 2. To divide every county into hundreds, of such size that all the children of each will be within reach of a central school in it. But this division looks to many other fundamental provisions. Every hundred . . . should be a corporation to manage all its concerns . . . as the selection of the Eastern townships. . . . These little republics would be the main strength of the great one. We owe to them the vigor given to our Revolution in its commencement in the Eastern States, and by them the Eastern States were enabled to repeal the embargo in opposition to the Middle, Southern, and Western States, and their large and lubberly divisions into counties which can never be assembled. General orders are given out from a centre to the foreman of every hundred, as to the sergeants of an army, and the whole nation is thrown into energetic action, in the same direction in one instant and as one man, and becomes absolutely irresistible.

PUBLIC LIBRARIES AND AN ACADEMICAL VILLAGE

Nothing would do more extensive good at small expense than . . . a small circulating library in every country, to consist of a few well-chosen books to be lent to the people . . . such as would give them a general view of other history and particular view of that of their own country, a tolerable knowledge of geography, the elements of natural philosophy, of agriculture and mechanics. . . . My services in this way are freely at . . . command.

No one more sincerely wishes the spread of information among mankind than I do, and none has greater confidence in its effect towards supporting free and good government. I am sincerely rejoiced, therefore, to find that so excellent a fund has been provided for this noble purpose in Tennessee. . . . I consider the common plan (for colleges) followed in this country, but not in others, of making one large and expensive building, as unfortunately erroneous. It is infinitely better to erect a small and separate lodge for each professorship, with only a hall below for his class and two chambers above for himself; joining these lodges by barracks for a certain portion of the students, opening into a covered way to give a dry communication between all the schools. The whole of these arranged around an open square of grass and trees would make it, what it should be in fact, an academical village. . . . Much observation and reflection on these institutions have long convinced me that the large and crowded buildings in which youths are pent up are equally unfriendly to health, to study, to manners, morals, and order.

SIMON BOLIVAR

This is the Story of Simon Bolivar,
Liberator of Venezuela, the Man
who first of all had the Vision
of a United States for the whole
of the American Continent.

SIMON BOLIVAR

In dedicating these pages
to
T. R. YBARRA
of Caracas and Harvard
I shall cheerfully overlook
the very embarrassing fact
that for more than thirty years
he has made his many friends
(the present one included)
feel deeply ashamed
that they could lay no claim
to having a single drop of the blood
of their South American neighbors
in their own lukewarm veins.

Foreword.

ONCE UPON A TIME—a great many years ago—I had a
professor who was not only a man of great learning but
also very much of a human being and therefore willing
to answer foolish questions. Now one day it so happened
that I asked him something about an historical detail
which failed to make sense to me.

"I am very sorry," he answered, "but I, too, am sadly
ignorant about the history of that country. And I really
ought to know. I suppose I ought to write a book about it
and learn."

He was right—dead right. The only way in which one
can really ever hope to understand a problem is by writing a book about it, and never has this become as clear to
me as during the time I had the pleasure of occupying
myself with Simon Bolivar.

Whenever people used to ask me whether I had any notion about the history of South America, I used to tell
them that yes, in a vague sort of way, I probably had a
general impression about what had happened there during the last four centuries. Today I know better. My ignorance was abysmal, and it was an abyss that had no
bottom. Even the names of many men who, each in their
own way, had played a rôle quite as important as that of
George Washington and Thomas Jefferson in our own

part of the world meant nothing to me. The fact that the South American continent had produced at least three George Washingtons against our one only began to dawn upon me after I was half way through with my manuscript and I had to begin all over again to get them into the right perspective, and I needed a year for a piece of work I had expected to do in a few months. Even now, after that year, I still tremble when I think of what may happen to me when my book is exposed to the criticism of the scholars of Venezuela or Colombia, the Argentine and Chile.

This ignorance I fear me, is shared by most of my fellow Americans. The history of France and England and Sweden and Switzerland holds no secrets for us, but when it comes to the history of Uruguay or Ecuador or Brazil (which is just a trifle larger than the United States) we hee and haw and quickly change the subject.

I therefore decided (while writing) to change the entire scope of this small volume. Instead of telling the reader only about Simon Bolivar, I also gave the general background of the Liberator's ceaseless labors on behalf of South American freedom and independence. In this way I hoped to make the people who live north of Curaçao understand that they are not the only nation on this continent with a noble and glorious past. If their ignorance, thus exposed, will only lead to a greater sense of humility, they may in the end come to realize that Simon Bolivar was no swashbuckling leader of hopeless charges nor a futile visionary but a man of practical common sense when, almost a century and a half ago, he

stated that there could be only one solution for our difficulties—the establishment of a UNITED STATES OF BOTH
THE AMERICAS.

HENDRIK WILLEM VAN LOON.

Nieuw Veere
Old Greenwich
Connecticut

Chapter I.

The Stage is Set for the Appearance of Our
Hero and as It is a Very Large Stage, this
Must be a Rather Long Chapter.

IT WAS the last day of May of the year 1498 and Columbus has set forth on that terrible third voyage of his from which he was to return in fetters, handcuffed like a common criminal and accused of every sort of crime from petty larceny to murder. But this dreadful climax to his glamorous career still lay hidden from him by three months of tireless searching during which period, as he hoped, the problem of a short cut to the real Indies would at last be solved. He himself would thereupon stand revealed as the greatest navigator of all time and the son of the Genoese wool carder was not exactly lacking in ambition.

And so, at the head of an imposing fleet of six enormous ships (which together measured almost as many tons as a medium sized modern tramp) he had set forth to accomplish his life's final ambition and give Europe a direct and convenient road to the wonderland of the East.

On July thirty-first of the same year, while trying to find a convenient spot to replenish his empty water casks, he had changed his course slightly towards the north and had come upon an island which no white man had ever seen before. It was dominated by three very high mountains and Columbus therefore called it the Island of the Holy Trinity or Trinidad.

Having filled his barrels with fresh water, he had again hoisted anchor and early in the morning of Wednesday, August first, had seen a bit of land which he mistook for still another island, which he called the Isla Santa or Holy Island. He had not bothered to explore this bit of land but had continued further towards the west convinced that now at last he was bound for that stretch of open sea that would carry him directly to Japan and China and the Indies.

Then something unexpected happened. Certain mysterious currents made their appearance, threatening the safety of his small squadron. Columbus, although an incorrigible dreamer who never quite understood the world in which he lived, was nevertheless one of the most experienced skippers of his day and age. He knew that such irregularities must be due to the fact that somewhere in that neighborhood a mighty river was losing itself in the ocean. No mere brook or rivulet could cause such a serious disturbance. But being in a hurry (as things were going none too well in near-by Hispaniola), he was unable to stop and investigate, in consequence whereof he never knew that he had sailed right past the mouth of the Orinoco River and that that little Isla Santa he had just placed on his map was really no island at all but part of that mighty South American continent, the existence of which he had suspected for quite a long time but which he had never been able to locate with absolute certainty.

Please remember the day. It was on Wednesday, August first, of the year 1498, that the Admiral of All the Oceans noted down in his log the fact that that morning, in the distance, he had caught sight of a little island, which he had called Isla Santa but he had not bothered to sail around it. As we now know, it was on that day that the continent of South America definitely entered into the destiny of the White Race, for Columbus had seen part of the coast of Venezuela.

The latter half of the fifteenth century and the first half of the sixteenth were eras of tremendous activity within the realm of discovery, exploration, and exploitation. The boom started the day the people of Europe heard of the fabulous wealth that awaited their pleasure on the other side of the ocean. Gold, silver, precious stones of all kinds were said to be there in such abundance that no one could fail to get rich. All one had to do was to take a chance. And soon every adventurer who could beg, borrow or steal a few thousand dollars was negotiating for the purchase of a leaky old tub. Next he was hiring a couple of greedy scoundrels, also looking for a chance at some "easy money."

Then came the problem of finding a pilot, but as everybody claimed that he had made at least one trip, that detail offered no serious difficulties. Then the voyage could begin.

The history books of these exciting years relate (though without any trace of wonder) that the great majority of those candidates for undeserved riches came to

*The white man's first landing on the coast of the new world.
Is there gold in this sand?*

a bad end. They were either caught by the Spanish authorities and hanged as common poachers, or their self-styled "pilot" ran their vessel on a rock and drowned not only himself but also most of his shipmates. Or, if they actually succeeded in reaching "the Indies" (for the fable that these West Indian Islands were a part of the real Indies persisted for more than a century), they found nothing more profitable than a lot of sand and counted themselves fortunate if they were able to survive until by chance some other brigand of the high seas came along and gave them a passage home.

All this was common knowledge but just the same, a few—a very few—of these gamblers had been exceptionally lucky and had lived to tell the tale. One day, when everyone had long since given them up as lost, they reappeared in Seville or in Palos, resplendent in beautiful new garments and closely followed by a small army of evil-looking retainers who carried mysterious boxes, said to be full of gold and precious stones.

The others, who had been less courageous, looked at them with hungry and envious eyes and in spite of the slender chances of success, they too a few days later could have been found in some cheap wineshop along the water front where some one (for a consideration) had promised to introduce them to a friend of his, a marvelous ocean pilot, who only the week before was said to have returned from a voyage during which he had met an old Indian who had told him about a region, not far from the coast, where there were cities made of solid gold and where the streets were made of solid silver and where the women were as beautiful as the houris of the Moslem's

Paradise. And although that pilot, when he had finally made his appearance, had proved to be a sodden old derelict who had never been within a thousand miles of the enchanted islands, the temptation proved too great and the old vagabond had been hired then and there and at an outrageous salary, with a fifty per cent bonus of everything that was to be found.

A month later and still another thirty-ton pinnace, manned by a dozen desperadoes, was madly bobbing on the waves of the turbulent Atlantic and another expedition was on its way to fortune or perdition.

Just the same, these desperate ventures served a good purpose, for even if only one-tenth of those fortune seekers returned to tell their stories, the oddly assorted scraps of information they brought home, when duly classified and sifted by the careful and efficient mapmakers of Lisbon and Seville, were bound to add further details to whatever was already known about the New World, and in that way, the little Isla Santa kept growing and growing until half a century after the death of Christopher Columbus, practically the whole outline of the new continent had been located and described. As it was the biggest piece of solid land which had ever been discovered, the Spanish crown decided that the time had undoubtedly come to take official cognizance of its existence and to take such measures as were necessary to be sure that all possible profits should flow into the empty coffers of the hungry Spanish treasury and into those of private citizens, most of whom only existed because the hangman had been a bit careless when he adjusted the rope to their necks.

Then at last there was an end to the haphazard system of highway robbery of the great conquistadores—the Pizarros and the Cortezes and all those other savages who, having started life as possibly swineherds or mule drivers, treated the natives in the same way they had formerly treated their four-legged charges and who stole and plundered with such happy abandon that, if they had been given their way, soon the continent of South America would have been completely drained of its gold and silver and also of its native inhabitants.

Once this decision to take official action had been reached, noble Spanish hidalgos were duly appointed as viceroys of these distant domains and they and their families solemnly crossed the ocean, solemnly moved into the stately palaces that had been prepared for them, and with an even greater degree of solemnity proclaimed themselves as the living symbols of royal authority.

That was the beginning of a new era. The period of leaving those rich territories to the mercies of the explorer, the conquistador, and the freebooter had come to an end. From then on, the New World was to obey the will of the man who as "I, the King" was the undisputed master of practically one-third of the entire globe.

A few years ago in the city of New York I had the honor of meeting the last direct descendant of *Yo, el Rey*. He was an agent for an automobile factory and I was thinking of buying a new car. It was an interesting experience. The young man's great-great-grandfather had had the right to burn my own great-great-grandfather at the stake, had he been rash enough to trespass on his property anywhere south of Curaçao. When the descendant of Yo, el Rey and I started upon our negotiations, I could tell him quite casually and without fear for my head that he was too expensive and that I could do better elsewhere.

Such far-reaching changes don't just happen. They are the results of centuries of lack of intelligence and incessant errors of judgment. Of these I shall now tell you and in as few words as possible.

Every story has got to have its beginning and for the sake of greater convenience, I shall begin with that date which is familiar to even the humblest contestants in the "Take it or leave it" program. I shall start out with those exciting years when Columbus stumbled upon those islands which until the end of his days he supposed to be part of the Indies and of China and Japan.

Columbus had accomplished his feat by sailing due west. The western road was therefore closed to the Portuguese, who during the previous hundred and fifty years had been the leaders within the field of discovery. But there was nothing to prevent them from trying their luck by making use of the eastern approach. Under the leadership of Prince Henry the Navigator, they had laid their plans most carefully. During the fourteenth century they had established themselves among the Azores and in Madeira. Using those islands as a sort of springboard, they had thereupon worked their way southward until in the year 1488 a certain Bartholomeu Diaz had found the Cabo Tormentoso, which later navigators, who had not found it quite so stormy, rebaptised the Cape of

Good Hope.

Eleven years after Diaz's unsuccessful attempt to round this cape and lose himself in the Indian Ocean, another Protuguese by the name of Vasco da Gama finally solved this problem and after a short and uneventful voyage in an eastern direction, he reached the shores of the Indian peninsula not far away from the city of Calicut. The Portuguese thereupon established an empire of their own in this part of the world and soon they were reaping so rich a harvest that it almost surpassed the profits which the Spaniards were gathering in from their gold and silver mines in Mexico and Peru.

The exploration fever was then at red heat and in every part of the world the Spaniards and the Portuguese were beginning to fight each other for the spoils. Another dozen years and everywhere Christians would be slaying Christians for the sake of mere material gain. This seemed a great pity to His Holiness, the Pope. Surely the two nations which were among the most faithful sons of the Church should not be allowed to kill each other when there was treasure enough in this world to make everybody rich. If each one of these two peoples (so the Church sensibly reasoned) could be persuaded to stick to its own sphere of influence, then there would be peace between them and there would be an end to this disastrous struggle which in reality was a war between brothers.

With this noble thought in mind, Pope Alexander VI (a Spaniard by the name of Rodrigo Borgia) had in the year 1493 taken a ruler and had carefully divided the

Carefully divided the map of the world into two equal parts.

map of the world into two equal parts. His line of demarcation, decided upon at a conference in the Spanish town of Tordesillas and therefore known as the Line of Tordesillas (a sort of mediaeval Mason and Dixon line) ran in such a manner that all the territory from several hundred miles inland in Brazil up to the western half of Japan became Portuguese, while the rest of America (with the exception of that little piece of Brazil) and the whole of the Pacific Ocean were surrendered to the Spaniards. For further details, please consult the map.

Today, with the exception of a few odds and ends of

117

useless pieces of real estate in Africa and Asia, not a square foot of these empires remains in the hands of the original owners. Trouble started almost as soon as this formal division had been made. The English and the Dutch pretended that they had never heard of this arrangement which had been made without their being considered, and they started to take whatever they pleased. The French and even the Swedes did likewise, and a few hundred years later, what still remained of these imperial domains declared itself free. But for the moment—that is to say during the first half of the sixteenth century—the Treaty of Tordesillas accomplished what the Pope had wanted it to do. It put an end to the rivalry between the Spaniards and the Portuguese and thereafter each country was able to devote itself undisturbedly to the exploitation, administration and maladministration of its recently acquired territories in Africa, Asia, and on the continent of America.

And this is the way the Spaniards arranged their own sphere of influence in the New World. They were not interested in the northern half. They knew that it existed, but a series of disastrous voyages into the hinterland had convinced them that it was a "land of no importance whatsoever" (as they used to express it so quaintly on their maps) and most likely would never be of any value to anybody.

But the southern half—that was a very different story! There among the mountains of the forbidding Andes gold and silver were at the disposal of any one able to make some one else pick them up for him. And whereas the northern half was only sparsely inhabited, the southern half had an abundant supply of natives who could be forced to work in the mines and on the plantations of the new owners.

The *dorados,* or gold lands, of Mexico and South America therefore became the center of the Spanish administration in the New World and for the sake of greater convenience this part of the globe was divided into two viceregencies, that of Mexico and that of Peru. During the middle of the eighteenth century, two more were added, New Granada, which covered the northernmost part of the continent, and Buenos Aires, which took care of the southern half.

In the beginning, that is to say, during the first fifty years after the arrival of Columbus, the city of San Domingo had been used as a clearinghouse for all the different administrative offices. There the supreme court for the colonies, the so-called *Audiencia,* had been located and all the more important official business with the home country had also been obliged to go through this town. But as there was a sad lack of trained civil servants (if one had to starve, one could do so just as conveniently at home as three thousand miles away), the administrative machinery worked with shocking slowness and devastating incompetence, and most merchants who had to transact business in the New World preferred to entrust their interests to private agencies who were on the premises and who knew how to get things done by the simple process of bribing the clerks who had to provide the necessary documents.

From our modern point of view, it was a very unsatisfactory arrangement, but it was ideally suited to those who were at the head of the colonial office in the mother country. These officials were—like all of us—the product of their own background and that background happened to be the era of the outgoing Middle Ages. And so they shared the views of their neighbors that wealth (outside of the possession of land) consisted of gold and silver and precious stones and such other materials as you could tuck away in our strongbox or hide in the cellar. It never occurred to them that a colony might be a very convenient place to which to send your surplus population, for that surplus population would thereupon settle down, would raise valuable crops of something or other and would engage in trade with the rest of the world. This trade could then be taxed and in this way it would add to the national revenue. For them this would have been too complicated a line of reasoning. The overseas domains—so they would have told you—existed to enrich the country which owned them. One emptied them of their treasures as one plundered a conquered city and spent as little money on their administration as possible. And in order to do this, it was absolutely necessary to maintain the same methods as had been used in the beginning.

New experiments were therefore out of the question. If some way had been found that was fairly successful, one stuck to it through thick and thin and though in the meantime the world might have been completely changed, everything must continue to be done as it had always been done.

Occasionally it might happen that a viceroy or a minor official, endowed with a little more energy and insight than his colleagues, would denounce the system and suggest a much better way of doing business. Immediately all the others would gang up against him. He would be denounced in Madrid as a dangerous radical who had better be recalled and the moment he was gone (and invariably he went), everything would remain as it had always been before and the fate of the empire was left to the sloth and indifference of an army of employees most of whom had no incentive whatsoever to do more than what was asked of them and whose slogan for a successful career consisted of just two words, "Safety first!"

Of course, the colonial organizations of other nations were apt to show the same tendencies. This could hardly have been otherwise. The tropical climate was exhausting. Servants cost next to nothing. Time did not exist. The home government was far away and one ruled over a people who were absolutely without protection and whose native rulers had for thousands of years taught them to suffer without complaining. But in Spain, conditions were almost as bad. Due to its incredibly backward system of economics and the hopelessly inefficient government of a number of its kings, the Spanish national government went bankrupt twice. A national bankruptcy is a dreadful thing, as we know from recent experiences in Europe. It means that nobody who works for the state gets paid, and people with hungry families will help themselves to whatever they need when they cannot get it in a legitimate fashion.

After such periods of insolvency, the government used to go through short-lived periods of "reform" in order to put an end to the wholesale bribery that had made itself evident in every part of the colonies. But it never went down to the roots of the evil which prevented these overseas possessions from being as prosperous as they should have been and that evil was something which today we would call "absentee landlordism."

When conditions grew unbearable, the government would occasionally take a bold step in the right direction. Then it would establish a few new centers of administration or relieve the surpeme court of Santo Domingo by creating half a dozen other *Audiencias* to handle the local affairs of some of the more distant provinces. But never, during all these many centuries during which almost half of the world belonged to Spain, did Madrid think it necessary to send its Council of the Indies to the colonies that the members with their own eyes might see what was wrong and what should be done to bring about the necessary improvements.

It is quite true that a similar accusation could be made against the English who during the course of the eighteenth century became the exclusive owners of the greater part of North America. But in one respect the English were in a much more favorable position than their Spanish neighbors of the south. What was called New England was in reality a new England, a part of the old England bodily transplanted unto American soil, whereas the New Spain, which you will find engraved on the maps, was by no means a transplanted part of the old

There among the mountains time did not exist.

Spain but merely a piece of colonial property where the natives had learned to speak a few words of Spanish and had given up the unpleasant habit of making human sacrifices, but where for the rest, conditions remained very much as they had been before the arrival of the White Man. From a Spanish point of view, it might be argued that this showed that Spain was in a better condition than England. Spain had not been touched by the Reformation. There were no groups of dissenters who so greatly resented the form of government under which they were obliged to live that they had no other choice than to leave and start a new existence in a distant and different part of the globe. Such immigrants did not come to America to enrich themselves over night and then hasten back home. They came to stay and their sense of well-being and security gave them a spirit of freedom and self-reliance which gradually turned them into a new race, so that by the middle of the eighteenth century there were two kinds of Englishmen, those of the Old World and those of the New World. And when a series of mistakes on the part of the government in London forced the colonists to declare themselves independent and to set up in business for themselves as an independent nation, there were enough transplanted Englishmen and their descendants in the New World to make the venture a success.

In Spain, conditions had been very different. There, no political and religious upheavals had forced part of the population to go forth in search of a new home in another part of the world. It is true that Spain, during the sixteenth century, had expelled all its Jews, but these victims of the Nuremberg laws of the sixteenth century had, of course, been unable to go to America, where they would still have been at the mercy of the Inquisition. Most of them had fled to the Low Countries, as England, ever since the thirteenth century, had closed its doors to Jewish immigration and had not shown a more tolerant attitude towards these unfortunate fugitives until the days of Cromwell.

There remained the peasants and the craftsmen and the small merchants of the Iberian peninsula (the class of people who formed the bulk of the immigrants who came to our own shores) but they really had no sound reason to pull up stakes and go somewhere else. Their fields were barren and their lives were desperately hard, but they knew that they would be just as badly off in the New World as they had been in the old one. Worse, maybe, as the fields there had never been tilled before, as the climate was not at all suitable to the needs of the White Man and as the arrows of the invisible but omnipresent natives had been tipped with a deadly poison. And they realized, too, that unless they were well endowed with funds, they would never have the slightest chance at enriching themselves, for the only immigrants who did well in New Spain were those who either by cash or by royal favor had got hold of vast tracts of land which they were thereupon able to turn into plantations worked by slave labor.

And here I come upon a very unpleasant subject, a subject as old as the human race and as disastrous for the master as it is for the servant, but one that cannot be avoided, as it played much too important a role on both halves of our continent.

Here I have to make a confession. During a great many years, remembering the dreadful conditions which had prevailed in Santo Domingo during the rule of Columbus and the bestial cruelty displayed by many of the early conquistadores, I had shared the opinion, which still seems to be held by a great many people, that the Spaniards had been much more harsh in their dealings with the Indians than any other nation. I was wrong and I have since then learned differently. Undoubtedly the conditions prevailing in the Spanish colonies in America had, in the beginning at least, been inexcusably bad. But I should have remembered that Columbus had been an abject failure as a civil administrator, that his brother, who occasionally had substituted for him, had been just about as incompetent and that the city of Santo Domingo, in spite of its many churches, had been a sink of depravity, as it had attracted all the worst elements of the mother country. I also should have kept in mind the type of men who had conquered Mexico and Peru, a low crew of cutthroats and brigands, and to my own shame, I should have given a thought to the early arrivals on our own northern shores and how they had treated the natives, who as a rule had welcomed them with a naïve sort of decency and without whose kind assistance, a great many of our forefathers would have starved to death. But whereas the White Man of the north continued to exterminate his copper-colored brethren until there were no more than a handful left, and had done his slaughtering without even being taken seriously to task by his spiritual leaders, it is to the everlasting glory of the Spanish churchmen that they not only had the courage to speak out boldly against this barbarous system of dealing in human flesh but had done whatever they could to ameliorate the fate of these unfortunate redskins.

The terrible conditions prevailing in the New World in regard to the treatment of the natives were soon known in Europe and it was then that the Church made itself the champion of the rights of the Indians. These benighted heathen, so the Church argued, even if they went about naked and painted their faces as only the very finest ladies in Europe dared to do, were, after all, human beings and therefore had an immortal soul and a right to be taught the benefits of the Christian religion. Once persuaded of the errors of their old ways and willing to accept the tenets of the True Faith, they would enjoy the same chances at salvation as any other Christians, for St. Peter was not interested in cither race or color and asked for a very different kind of credentials from those that were demanded by the authorities who represented the majesty of the White Man's superiority.

As a result of those reports about the sad fate of the Red Man, who now had been deprived not only of house and home but also of his freedom, several shiploads of eager friars were soon crossing the ocean and once in the New World, these indefatigable apostles of the Christian faith penetrated into every nook and corner of the continent. It was they who in the end conquered it for the civilization of the old Spain, for they came in direct contact with the aborigines and though we cannot always understand their methods, we must give them credit for having accomplished what those bearing the sword could never have done and they made the New Spain a cultural part of the old one.

There was, for example, that curious state in the heart of the continent which was to become one of the most interesting experiments in statecraft of the last four thousand years. Alhough under the Crown of Spain, it really functioned as a quite independent community, founded and ruled over by the members of the Society of Jesus, or the Jesuits, as we usually call them. This vast territory, roughly covering the modern state of Paraguay and established in the year 1605, was so much better administered than the rest of the Spanish and Brazilian colonies that when after a century and a half (in the year 1750) the Jesuits were forced to surrender their holdings to the Portuguese of Brazil, the natives rallied right heartily to the support of their clerical leaders. This, however, did them little good. The combined forces of Spain and Portugal were too strong and the Jesuits were forced to surrender to the Portuguese. Whereupon (and in a surprisingly short period of time) the natives fell back into their old and highly reprehensible ways, all roads and villages disappeared, and Paraguay descended to the same low civil, moral, and economic level as was to be found in much of the rest of the continent.

There are other examples which give proof that the missionaries of the different orders which had hastened to South America took a most serious view of their duties as guardians and protectors of their copper-colored disciples and that they were infinitely more successful in dealing with the so-called "native problem" than the civilians who were sent out by the government. Not only did they have an inherent respect and love for their fellow men, no matter how humble, but their success probably was due in part to the fact that the Church was the only institution in ancient times which was familiar with that science which today is known to us as the science of applied psychology. Very few of these missionaries were supermen but that was not necessary for them in order to function intelligently. Even when they were simple, rustic fellows from the backwoods of Spain, they belonged to an organization which for fifteen entire centuries had been able to maintain itself because it had made such a close study of the human soul. These missionaries knew (or at least suspected) what made those who came to them for counsel and consolation click. It took them only a very short time to adapt the methods they had learned at home to the needs of their savage charges and their hold became so great upon them that even today, after an almost endless series of revolutions (some of which were decidedly anti-religious in their tendencies) the South American continent remains one of the staunchest bulwarks of the Catholic Church.

Many of these preachers of the Gospel were of Spanish peasant origin and from childhood on they had been taught to accept their monarchy as a divinely ordained institution which no good Christian should ever question.

This made them ideal subjects of the crown, which had little use for those liberal minds which were forever asking embarrassing questions, and even after most South American countries had set themselves free, some of these missionaries still remained loyal to the King of Spain. But with all their conservative tendencies and their unwillingness to risk new experiments, they stood—as human beings—head and shoulders above the rank and file of the other Spaniards who during the first half century after the discovery of America had hastened to the New World, and it was among these clerics that the first steps were taken to improve the fate of the unfortunate natives who, whenever they rose in rebellion, were thrown to the dogs or were drowned in their masters' fishponds.

Best known among those who took the side of the oppressed was the famous Bartolomé de las Casas who afterwards became known as the Apostle of the Indies. Las Casas had first come to Santo Domingo in 1498, only a few years after the city had been founded. He was then still in his twenties and was accompanied by his father. He went back to Spain but in 1502 he returned to Haiti where some time later he was ordained as a priest.

That was the beginning of his real life, for the next fifty years he spent in one effort after another to save his beloved Indian children from the brutalities to which they were submitted by his fellow Spaniards. He did his best to have laws passed which should protect the serfs of the *repartimientos* (the big estates of the rich landowners) against their Spanish masters. He caused a royal edict to be passed which forbade the further enslavement of those

Indians who were still free, and for a while he even presided over a short-lived model colony where the Indians were supposed to enjoy the same freedom as was afterwards (in the year 1822) bestowed upon the American Negro slaves who had been set free and had been taken back to Africa to live in the independent republic of Liberia.

In the pursuit of these most laudable activities, he traveled thousands of miles in miserable little ships, experienced every kind of hardship, was exposed to every variety of horrible diseases and invariably found himself at loggerheads with the civilian authorities. But until the very last he remained indefatigable in his efforts on behalf of the Indians and when he was already in his eighties he made a special trip to England because he had heard that the Spanish colonists in America had sent a petition to King Philip II (who then happened to be in London) with a request that he permit them to enslave all the natives in every part of both the Americas.

Now it so happened during the career of this great and good man that once upon a time, while he was presiding over a commission of Hieronymite Fathers, sent to the New World to look into the wrongs of the Indians, he let himself be persuaded that the best way to save the Indians from complete extermination was to let them be replaced by African Negroes. The dark-skinned Africans, as everybody knew, were a much hardier race than the light-skinned Indians. They could perform the hardest kind of manual labor and yet live for as long as ten or even twenty years, whereas the ordinary Indian laid himself down and died after only a couple of months in the mines or in the fields. After due deliberation, the Commission therefore declared in favor of this "humane and charitable arrangement," which would solve the problem of Indian slavery, and it is to that decision that we owe the introduction of Negro slavery onto the American continent.

Poor well-meaning but misguided Bartolomé de las Casas was to spend the rest of his days (he reached the age of ninety-two) being sorry for what he had done. For no sooner had the news reached Europe that African slaves could now be freely imported into every part of the Spanish-American possessions, than there was a new shipping boom. However, this time the vessels were not equipped for carrying ordinary merchandise but cargoes of human beings, and these black men and women, shackled together like animals, were exposed to such atrocious treatment that as a rule half of them died before they were halfway across the ocean.

The Portuguese, who were in control of Africa, were the first to avail themselves of this marvelous opportunity at getting rich with a minimum of labor. The Arabs did the really hard work connected with this nefarious trade. They went into the interior of the Black Continent and bought the necessary goods from the native rulers, who felt towards their subjects as the Landgraves of Hesse felt towards theirs during our revolution when they sold their peasants as soldiers to the English. Having gathered together a sufficient number of these pitiable black people, the Arabs next drove their herd to the coast where the Portuguese were waiting for them, cash in hand. And as soon as a ship had as much of a load as it could hold, it set sail for the Caribbean Sea, where the Spanish middleman looked after the further distribution.

The business, in spite of the terrific overhead on account of the loss of property through death, proved so profitable that almost at once every other nation tried to cut in, even if this meant a chance of being hanged by a Portuguese viceroy of the Ivory Coast or his subordinate in Angola.

The Dutch, I am ashamed to say, were among the first to go in for this new form of easy wealth and they were just as cruel in their treatment of the slaves as the Portuguese had been.

Eventually, almost every other nation of Europe engaged in such commerce and it was not until the beginning of the last century that an end was made to this ghastly business of stealing human beings and selling them for profit. Even then, it took the greater part of the British Navy a great many years to stop it and to rid the seas of the slave dealers, who by then were in the habit of drowning their living cargo in case they feared capture and detection.

The history of Spain in the New World does not always make pleasant reading. But the Spaniards, when confronted with some of the terrible things their ancestors did in the New World, can always answer: "You may be right in these accusations. You probably are right and it is a pity and a shame that they happened. But we had our Las Casas and we had him three centuries before you had yours."

Then with all these arguments in its favor, why is the story of Spanish rule in the New World a record of so much injustice and so much misery?

In history, as in daily life, there is never one single cause for anything that comes about. Towers do not suddenly crumble into dust. Empires do not perish over night. Families do not go into bankruptcy and ruin at twenty-four hours' notice. There are always a number of causes and each one of them contributes its own big or little share to the final disaster. But exactly how each one operates, it is often hard to detect or to define. So when I now try to set down a few of these contributing factors, I do so with considerable misgivings and the feeling that, no matter how hard I try to be fair, I may be wrong just the same.

One of the most important causes for the deplorable way in which the Spanish colonies lagged behind the rest of the world, I have already mentioned. That was the insistence of the home government on keeping everything that was being done in its own hands and in systematically stifling all effort at any kind of private initiative. Sometimes in following this policy, the Spanish crown went to almost unbelievable limits. For example, it would not allow the building of roads which would have made it possible for the people of the different parts of any given province to communicate with each other. This led to absolutely absurd results. It was, for example, much easier to travel from Cartagena (in present-day Colombia) to Seville or Cadiz in the old Spain than it was to proceed from Cartagena to some other port along the coast of the Caribbean Sea situated only a few hundred miles away.

This obstinate insistence upon the centralization of all power was also responsible for that hopeless lack of speed in the transaction of official business, which soon became an object of ridicule to the whole world. Twice a year— once in the spring and once in the fall—a large commercial fleet, heavily protected by vessels of war, would cross from Spain to America or vice versa and this armada would also carry the mail. But the colonial officials were so slovenly in answering the letters addressed to them that it often took years before there was a reply to a most urgent request for something that needed immediate attention and in a great many cases, the papers were so carefully pigeonholed that they remained forgotten for several hundred years.

In the second place, there were not sufficient inducements to make any great part of the Spanish people want to pull up stakes in the old homeland and try their luck in the New World. But there were also a great many other things which interfered with the normal development of South America and kept it from that economic and political place of importance to which it was entitled by both its size and its natural wealth.

The chronic state of semi-bankruptcy with which the Spanish Government had to wrestle during the sixteenth and seventeenth centuries made it extremely difficult to maintain a sufficient number of soldiers and sailors to protect these vast territories against the attacks of

Spain's manifold enemies. These thousands of miles of coast were an easy prey to any enterprising buccaneer who was willing to run the slight risks of being caught and hanged, and realizing that they could not hold their seaports against the English and Dutch pirates of the Caribbean, the Spanish Government ordered that all the provincial capitals should be established at a safe distance from the sea, so that they should no longer be exposed to unexpected raiding expeditions.

This made for greater security but was, of course, a most inconvenient arrangement. It meant that all merchandise destined for the mother country (and no other trade was allowed) must first be unloaded at the mouth of a river, must then be carried several hundred miles inland, and must there be stored until a homebound fleet was ready to take care of it. Then once more it had to be hoisted onto the backs of men and beasts for the exhausting return trip to the coast. Try and do business in the face of such handicaps!

And now a final reason why these incredibly rich lands never reached that state of prosperity to which they were entitled. When sometimes we express surprise at the deep-seated differences that seem to exist between the civilizations of South America and North America, we should remember that compared to ourselves, South America is already very old. There was a beginning of Spanish culture in South America long before our own ancestors appeared in Boston and New Amsterdam. South America is full of churches and public buildings that were built more than a hundred years before Henry Hudson

But nothing much ever happened between armadas.

discovered Coney Island and mistook the mouth of the river now called after him for a short cut to the Pacific.

Now during that century and a half of almost complete isolation, it had been possible for quite a new kind of Spanish civilization to establish itself among the remote valleys of this sparsely populated region. I stress this fact because we have got to keep it well in mind if we want to understand the difficulties which Simon Bolivar had to overcome when he set out to bring liberty unto all the people of the South American continent.

George Washington (and heaven knows, he had difficulties enough of his own trying to keep only thirteen small colonies together) was dealing with a more or less homogenous mass of people, whereas Bolivar was obliged to handle as motley a crowd as was ever assembled underneath a single banner.

To mention these different groups and classes according to the role they were to play in Bolivar's activities, there was, first of all, the class of the so-called Creoles. They were the descendants of the white people who centuries before had come to South America and who for one reason or another had decided to settle down there. In the beginning, the Spanish authorities had dreamed of creating a new and truly South American "people" by encouraging marriages between the white immigrants and the daughters of native chieftains. But such unions had rarely been successful. The Indians (even those of Mexico and Peru, where they were supposed to have established a kind of civilization of their own) were still pretty close to a state of almost complete savagery and, especially in their love for human sacrifices, they were but a few steps removed from their ancestors of the early Stone Age.

This effort, therefore, to provide the South American continent with a new class of inhabitants that should be a mixture of the old natives and of imported Europeans was doomed to failure from the start. The Indians seem to have realized this even sooner than the White Man, and not caring in the least for the civilization of their new masters, they hastened to lose themselves among the endless forests of the interior and were never seen again.

But what of the other white immigrants who were not used for such interesting experimental purposes? There were not a great many of them but during such a long period of years it was unavoidable that at least a few should have found their way to the New World. Most of them, especially in the beginning, had undoubtedly come in the vague hope of making at least a competence and then being able to return to the mother country and live in modest comfort. But most of them, like the movie-struck boys and girls who today trek to Hollywood, had never earned the price of a return ticket and had therefore been obliged to stay where they were, finding whatever employment was offered them and making the best of a most disheartening bargain.

The few who had done a little better had invested their money in local real estate and had become small-scale plantation owners, for the big haciendas were only within reach of the very rich. Being left to their own devices and with very little direct contact with the mother country, these permanent settlers had gradually developed certain social and economic standards of their own. After a couple of centuries their way of living had become so rigidly characteristic that their civilization was almost as different from that of the old Spain as that of a Connecticut Yankee was different from that of a Yorkshireman or the culture of the French part of Canada was different from that of the Ile de France.

I am not merely talking now of the less fortunate ones who had never even risen above some humble craft and who had long since realized that they would always have to eke out a miserable existence as shoemakers or bakers or butchers or sextons or schoolmasters. The poor have always been out of luck and it made very little difference whether these miserable creatures sweltered in the slums of Porto Cabello or in those of Madrid. But it was the spirit of the times which accepted it as an established fact that the vast majority of all people had been born for the express purpose of waiting on their betters and these unfortunate creatures were too ill-fed and too much afflicted with disease and too broken in spirit ever to dream of rising against the powers that held them in their hopeless state of servitude. That class of society therefore—the lower middle class—was out as potential revolutionary material.

It is undoubtedly true that every successful revolution is at times in need of a mob. But the crowd plays only a secondary role, like the chorus in an opera. When you have not had quite enough to eat for six or eight generations, you are not apt to feel energetic enough to brave the terrors of marching against well-trained, well-fed battalions of policemen or soldiers. Therefore, the real leaders of almost every revolution have belonged to the higher classes of society. Invariably the initiative was taken by men in whom economic security and a sense of superiority (maintained for generations) had bred that spirit of independence and defiance which had made them willing to take the risks which are the inevitable part of defying the machine guns of those in power.

Our own revolution is an example of what I mean. The commander-in-chief of the armies of the thirteen Colonies was also the richest man of the North American continent. Jefferson was a prosperous landowner. Thrifty Benjamin Franklin had done pretty well for the son of a Boston soap-boiler. The Adamses were very comfortably off. Jimmy Madison's father was not exactly rich but he could afford to send his son to Princeton. And it was the flower of Europe's nobility which hastened across the ocean to offer its sword to this interesting experiment in applied democracy.

In France, too, the leaders who actually started the revolution belonged almost exclusively to the classes that had known a certain amount of comfort and leisure and it was only after they had withdrawn from the scene that the rabble had its chance. The rebellion of the Netherlands against Spain was led by a prince of the blood and even our humble friend, Lenin, was by no means a proletarian (as so many people still seem to believe) for he belonged to the lower nobility of old Imperial Russia. Cromwell, who overthrew the rule of the Stuarts in England, was a Cambridge graduate and the descendant of a man who had married the sister of one of the ministers of Henry VIII, a certain Thomas Cromwell, and who had been so proud of this illustrious union that he had dropped his original name of Williams and had adopted that of Cromwell. And no one will ever pretend that Franklin Delano Roosevelt, who led that serious economic upheaval of a few years ago, now known as the New Deal, was exactly a product of New York's slums.

I could continue the list for several more pages but these few examples will show what I mean. It takes courage and determination and independence of thought and action to upset a system of government or economics that has been accepted for two or three or sometimes a dozen centuries as being something absolutely perfect, and such courage and determination are not apt to be found among those who do not know what it means to have their tummies full of food and who have been trained from childhood to show a decent respect to those whom John Adams called, "The rich, the well-born and the able."

In a few more moments I shall introduce you to our hero, young Simon Bolivar.* He, too, was scion of one of the most powerful clans of South America. This, however, did not make him an aristocrat in the eyes of the officials whom Spain sent out to administer her possessions in the New World. The fact that he had been born on American soil made him a Creole and even the best among the Creoles were only second-best in the eyes of a Spaniard who had been born in Spain and who expected

* Símon Bolívar (Seé-mon Bo-leé-var)

to return to the old country the moment he had done his turn of service.

This led to a curious social arrangement, very uncomfortable and quite humiliating for the native-born citizens but one we can understand, for the exact equivalent existed in our own part of the world. As was only natural, a great many of these native-born families had increased in wealth to a point at which they were much better bred and lived much more luxurious lives than the Spanish officials who were supposed to rule them and who used every occasion to make them feel that they were of an inferior social position.

The native-born returned the compliment by priding themselves on their riches. They could afford comforts that were entirely beyond the means of the Spanish administrators. Their children were better educated, for whenever it was possible to do so, the sons of these local dynasties had been sent to a European university to get a better training than was available at home. Their daughters and wives still lived according to those rules which had first been laid down in the second chapter of *Timothy* and they continued to be taught that it was woman's duty to behave in silence and with subjection, that she must never under any circumstances try to usurp authority over man but must dwell in silence and behave in all things with faith, charity, and holiness.

It need not be stressed that these rich young ladies were very apt to overlook the Pauline command that they appear in public with shamefacedness and sobriety and not with braided hair or gold or pearls or costly array. They knew that their fathers could afford to give them rich dowries and they were just as eager to follow the latest dictates of the leading couturiers of Paris as their sisters in any other part of the world. Most of the time they were still as carefully guarded as the inmates of a Turkish harem or a mediaeval castle, but they were gay and carefree young children and they meant to get out of life all there was to be got and if the only road to comparative personal liberty was by means of contracting an advantageous marriage—very well! They would marry the men their papas and mammas, their grandparents and uncles and aunts, had chosen for them and, having in this way gained a certain amount of freedom, they would arrange their lives as best suited them.

Quite naturally, it was among this class of society, among these well-to-do natives, of Spanish descent but excluded from all active participation in the government, that three was the greatest amount of rebellion against the established order of things. No matter how rich and intelligent or powerful they might be within their own bailiwicks, they realized that they would always be doomed to play second fiddle and they did not like it.

I have mentioned something very much like this in my recent book on Thomas Jefferson. The old and established settlers of the northern half of the American continent smarted under exactly that same sort of feeling of inferiority, only in their case the superior race consisted of British instead of Spanish officials. Even George Washington, as patient and long-suffering a-mortal as ever lived, would occasionally lose patience when he, the commander of a provincial regiment which had just saved a regular officer of the King's forces from the disastrous results of his own incompetence, was exposed to the supercilious remarks of some absurd little lieutenant of the regular army. And Thomas Jefferson, who almost always accepted whatever came his way with supreme philosophic calm, is known to have flown into an occasional rage when, for example, he noticed how in London the representatives of the independent and sovereign United States of America were looked down upon as if they were something the cat had dared to bring into the Royal Presence.

Now this sort of class differentiation was comparatively harmless as long as the feeling of irritation was restricted to a single small group of society. But the whole world was changing and it was changing very rapidly. Under the leadership of the French philosophers of the eighteenth century, the spirit of man was everywhere awakening. The newly proclaimed and startling doctrines about the rights of man and about human freedom and equality for all did not fit into the scheme of things as conceived by that Bourbon dynasty which early during the eighteenth century had succeeded the Habsburgs on the throne of Spain. They were very much afraid that these dangerous radical doctrines might some day even find their way across the broad Atlantic and that such opinions might cause serious difficulties if they were to be accepted by a large part of the native-born Spanish settlers.

Of course, there was no immediate danger. It still took a copy of the French *Encyclopédie* (the handbook of general enlightenment of the eighteenth century) a great deal of time to cross the southern Atlantic. But even the Bourbons realized that ideas will travel in spite of all efforts~to the contrary and that then there would be an end to a system of intellectual, social, and economic sabotage in which the royal government followed but a single aim—to keep everything as it always had been, to oppose every form of change and to fill the jails with those who dared to maintain that the world doth move.

That, good reader, was the state of affairs when our hero, Simon Bolivar, appeared upon the stage. Outwardly, to be sure, everything was indeed as it had always been. The king was on his throne. The viceroy was in his vice-regal palace. The alcalde was in the city hall. The bishop supervised his diocese and his subordinates obeyed their bishop. The schoolteacher disciplined his pupils. The baker baked bread and the candlestick maker made candlesticks. The hangman took care of those entrusted to his ministrations and the rain rained with complete impartiality upon both the good and the evil.

But inwardly a new spirit was at work—that spirit which was born out of a rapidly increasing feeling of irrepressible irritation with the outworn and outgrown ideals of a bygone age, and which, for lack of a better name, I would like to call the spirit of America.

Chapter II.

A Rich Young Man with an Unfortunate Habit
of Asking Questions for Himself.

SIMON BOLIVAR was born on July 24th of the year 1783, the same year in which England and the United States of America concluded and signed the Treaty of Peace of Paris, which established us definitely as a free and independent nation. He died in the year 1830, shortly after Andrew Jackson had been elected to the presidency of the United States. His span of life therefore was a short one, only forty-seven years. But when, exhausted from the gruelling hardships of his many years in the field, and having lost all faith in the future, he closed his eyes with the desperate remark, "If only my death can help where my life has failed!" his work had been done.

He himself, seeing chaos all around him, might actually have come to believe that "those who have toiled for South American freedom have but plowed the sea," but posterity does not agree. The freedom of our sister nations of the south was the fulfillment of the dream of this brilliant son of Venezuela.

His contemporaries may not always have understood him and on many occasions their lack of vision and their own personal ambitions undoubtedly frustrated his plans for their happiness and his dream of a greater America. But what of it? Unless we take a long view of history, we are like scientists who look at the animal life of a drop of water as revealed by a microscope and forget about the existence of the ocean. It is true that Bolivar, who thought and acted in terms of the whole of South America and who detested the "parish politics" of the rest of the men with whom he had to deal, bestowed freedom upon only a small part of the continent. But once he had hoisted the banner of freedom, it was never again pulled down. And while he himself, during the agonizing last days of his life, may have looked back upon his career as a futile gesture and an out-and-out failure, we know better. We honor George Washington as the man who founded a single nation. Simon Bolivar bestowed independence upon half a dozen.

The hero of our story was an honest man and if he were asked to give a short account of himself for *Who's Who* or the *Congressional Record*, he probably would write something like this:

"I was born with a dozen golden spoons in my mouth. I also held a couple of them in each hand. As a child, I enjoyed the benefits of wealth and social position and I never had to give a thought to the day of tomorrow. I married a rich girl and when I went to Europe, both the Pope and the King of Spain were delighted to receive me. It is true that afterwards I lost all my possessions and quite often had to go without enough to eat or without the certainty of finding a roof over my head. But I made this sacrifice of my worldly goods deliberately and willingly. I therefore do not see that there was anything very praiseworthy in what people have sometimes called my 'noble gesture,' when they mean that I gave up all my worldly goods for the benefit of that fame which since then has become associated with my name.

"I am no fool. I understand the value of money. I realize the importance of having one's own home where one can raise one's own family and receive one's friends. But like the great Thomas Jefferson, whom, much to my regret, I never met in the flesh, I have all my lifelong days been a passionate lover of freedom and I would have felt very unhappy, sitting in slippered ease while my country was at the mercy of a government that was decidedly not of my own choosing.

"I treated the supercilious governors who were sent out to represent the Majesty of Spain with a deep-seated contempt and once we had achieved our liberty, I (again like that great American of the North, Thomas Jefferson) steadfastly fought the idea that the ruler of our republic should be called a king, and though I myself might have borne that title, I only wanted to be known and remembered as the Liberator, considering this token of approval on the part of my fellow citizens as the highest praise that could possibly be bestowed upon any human being.

"I am deeply concerned that I was not able to accomplish all the many things I had hoped to do, but like a faithful soldier, I died loyal to my principles, those same principles I had made my own when as quite a young man I climbed to the top of Rome's Sacred Mountain,

149

where during the glorious era of the old Republic the common people had gathered together to assert their rights against the aggressive pretentions of an arrogant and decaying aristocracy."

This little speech is, of course, fictitious but the incident to which the last sentence refers actually took place and it is as good a starting point for the telling of Bolivar's life story as any other. What has happened to other men of vision, influencing them in a way that has caused them to change the whole course of history—seems to have occurred to young Simon Bolivar when in the summer of the year 1805 he paid a visit to the Mons Sacra, just outside of Rome's Porta Pia.

He had not gone there alone. He had been accompanied by the inevitable private tutor, who was as much part of a young man of fashion making "the grand tour" as his letter of credit. In this case, the private tutor was a figure out of Dickens. From the descriptions we have of him by his contemporaries, he would have been an ideal addition to the brave band of explorers who ventured forth with the Hon. Samuel Pickwick when he undertook his famous voyage of discovery of a century ago and made the acquaintance of Mr. Samuel Weller and a great many other delightful characters who frequented the English countryside in the days of the coach and four.

The name of the little man was Simon Rodriguez. He was suspected of "radical leanings," for he was an eager disciple of the great French philosophers of the eighteenth century and an enthusiastic believer in the rights of man, in human liberty, in human equality and in all those other dangerous doctrines which were held in particular abhorrence by the really nice people. Not that the rich plantation owners of South America had as yet experienced any direct reactions from the terrible things that were happening to their aristocratic friends in France. But they had carefully perused the Madrid papers, which had not overlooked any of the more gruesome details connected with this great historical event, and they had been horrified at what they had read. Being unable to act, they had prayed for that good King Louis, so cruelly put to death by his wicked subjects, and wept copious and sincere tears over the fate of his lovely and innocent consort. They had welcomed those who had been fortunate enough to escape from the holocaust and had tried to be nice to them, though they had found them to be sadly lacking in the more serious aspects of life as it was still being lived in this remote and sleepy part of the Spanish overseas possessions. And they had thanked their saints that they resided so far from this cesspool of iniquity that such things as were common events in France could never happen to them on their safe haciendas.

That the education of young Simon should have been entrusted to one deeply and darkly suspected of Jacobin sympathies (at that time anybody whose ideas one did not like was denounced as a Jacobin, just as today we call him a Red) was something which made very little sense and undoubtedly many of the uncles and aunts of young Simon predicted that no good would come of it. But the particular uncle who had been made the guardian of the young Bolivar children after their parents' death was at his wits' end and as Rodriguez seemed the first teacher who could handle his difficult ward, he had been careful not to ask any embarrassing questions but had hired him then and there and had told him to try and see what he could do with this recalcitrant infant.

Today we would have called Simon a "problem child" and we would have sent for the school psychologist. But in the year 1793 psychology had not yet been invented and the best one could do was to send for the village priest. Young Simon listened to this good and holy man— and serenely continued to live the kind of life that suited him, which was to do exactly as he pleased. That would hardly do for a gentleman of his tender years who some day would be one of the richest landowners of the whole of New Granada. He must at least have the rudiments of a polite education, but until then he had obstinately refused to wear any kind of pedagogical harness and there was the danger that in the end he would run completely wild, and wild young men with barrels of money at their disposal are very dangerous to the peace and quiet of the community in which they happen to live.

We now understand that there was really nothing very wicked about little Simon. He was merely bored by the succession of stupid private tutors who had been hired to teach him his three R's. He was so much brighter than any of them that he despised them and treated them like the blackamoors who were supposed to look after his physical needs.

Contempt of the pupil for the master will never bring about that feeling of respect and confidence which, ever since the beginning of time, has been the basis of all successful teaching, so little Simon therefore was running completely wild and in grave danger of developing into a ne'er-do-well. His guardian, an amiable but easygoing gentleman of leisure, soon grew tired of this continual fight between his nephew and his tutors and when at last he found someone who seemed to have an influence over the child, he hired him and considered himself fortunate that now he had done his duty and could return to his own pursuits.

As for the teacher who was to play such an important role in the life of his young charge, his name, as I said, was Simon Rodriguez and at the time he had that windfall of being engaged by one of the most prominent families of Venezuela; he was holding a very small position in the Department of Education in Caracas. At the moment Master Bolivar had just entered upon his fourteenth year. His father's name (a fact I should have mentioned before) was Juan Vicente Bolivar y Ponte. His mother, before her marriage, had been Maria de la Concepcion Palacios y Blanco. Both of them were of old Spanish stock but they belonged to families which had lived in South America for a great many generations and therefore were excluded from all direct participation in the government.

Senor Bolivar and his charming but ailing wife lived the usual life of people of their class. Part of the year they spent on their estate of San Mateo, out in the country, but as behooved their position as leading members of the local aristocracy, they also had a house in the city of Caracas, that they might occasionally be seen in the capital and keep up their social contacts.

Doña Maria, the wife of Don Juan, had had a hard time bearing her children. She was not very strong, had weak lungs, and since she rarely drew a breath of fresh air (fresh air not being considered "nice" for a lady of such elevated rank), she grew steadily worse. But being very much part of the world into which she had been born (the Spanish colonial world of the eighteenth century), she knew that women must not expect too much happiness in this world and was contented with her lot.

A curious story has come down to us about the baptism of our hero. Undoubtedly it was invented at a later date, when Bolivar had grown to be the greatest man of his race and was rapidly becoming a myth. According to this amiable phantasy, Don Juan had desired that his son be called San Iago, for it was the name-day of that saintly personage who not only happened to be the saint of the city of Caracas but also of the people of Spain. But the priest who was to officiate had objected to doing his bidding. "Some day," this venerable cleric had declared, "this baby will be like Simon Maccabaeus, who delivered the Jews from their foreign bondage. He too will bring freedom to his people, and therefore I shall baptise him Simon."

Now it not only seems most unlikely that a simple parish priest should have dared to speak in such a fashion to one who belonged to "the quality," but furthermore, in such matters the Church always respects the good right of parents to choose as they please. We therefore need not pay very much attention to what is undoubtedly a fable. As for Simon's contemporaries, if they had ever heard the story they would merely have shrugged their shoulders and would have answered you, "What does it matter? The child is so weak and puny, it won't live long anyway."

There is little to report about the first years of the future Liberator except that he survived the pills and purges of the Caracas chirurgeons and that he loved to play with his toy soldiers. In both these respects he was entirely like all other normal boys, who live to a ripe old age, once they have survived the common ailments of childhood, but who never again touch a gun unless they are afflicted with a desire to kill rabbits for the sake of sport. In a way, Simon's mother's weak constitution, which he had inherited, proved to be a blessing in disguise, for instead of being forced to live in stuffy dignity in the city of Caracas, he was allowed to run wild on the family estate of San Mateo and there is no better school (except for the acquisition of a little "book learnin'") than a farm. It may well be (though this is merely a guess on my part, for one can never be quite certain about such early influences) that life among the lowly slaves of the family estate opened Simon Bolivar's eyes at a very early age to the terrible conditions that prevailed among the workers on his father's hacienda. For, of course, he must have spent a great deal of his time in the slave quarters, which undoubtedly were much gayer than his own home, which was run like a hospital, what with a sick woman and the everlasting need of quiet and "Hush, hush, children! Mother is asleep."

When that happened, young Simon took out his horse (he had learned to ride at the age of eight) and gaily galloped off to his black friends, who adored him and always called him "the little master" and who, I suppose, compared him most favorably with the old master, who does not seem to have shared his son's liberal attitude towards "the problem of color."

Simon lost his father at a very early age, which meant that thereupon he was given even greater personal liberty than before and could do almost exactly as he pleased. After her husband's death, his mother withdrew more and more into that dark room where she could feel the presence of her favorite saints, until that sad day when Doña Maria, feeling her strength waning rapidly, asked to be carried to Caracas, there to await the end which she knew to be unavoidable.

She never saw her children again. She died of consumption in the month of July of the year 1792 and the two boys and the girls were entrusted to the care of their relatives. Simon went to live with his uncle, the aforementioned Don Carlos Palacios, while his elder brother, Juan, and his sisters found a different home. They remained, however, on very friendly terms and one of the sisters especially was to be of great help to Simon during the more desperate years of his later career.

Soon brother Juan was considered old enough to learn the business of running an estate and he thereupon returned to San Mateo. The sisters were being prepared for marriage, which was the only career open to the daughters of such a genteel family, and the chapter of the Bolivar orphans would have closed as such chapters almost invariably did, except for that curious twist in this young Simon Bolivar's character which had always set him apart from plain, ordinary, normal children and which from the very beginning seems to have destined him for a fate of his own.

Uncle Carlos, as I have already told you, had experienced great difficulties in finding the right kind of a teacher until in despair he had availed himself of the services of some one who had been recommended to him as a brilliant scholar and scientist but suspected of serious leanings towards the "radical" theories of the Revolution.

This dangerous "Red," Simon Rodriguez by name, was of obscure parentage but, like his pupil, he was a faithful and self-confessed disciple of Jean Jacques Rousseau, the Frenchman who had discovered "Natural Man." He recognized but one teacher and that teacher was no one less than Mother Nature herself. That mother, however, had not been very kind to her son when she endowed him with his physical attributes, for he was short and stocky and so nearsighted and awkward in all his movements that he looked like a caricature of himself. Being as poor as a church mouse, he had got into the habit of wearing any kind of clothes, usually a collection of assorted garments which charitable friends had passed on to him. In addition to this scarecrow appearance, he made himself look even more bizarre by refusing to wear shoes, for primitive man had gone barefoot and it therefore behooved a disciple of Jean Jacques Rousseau to do likewise. When either the conventions of the day or the heat of the city's pavements forced him to affect some kind of footgear, he put on a pair that were half a dozen sizes too large. But why bother about such an absurd trifle when the acquisition of a better fitting pair of boots would have consumed time he might have put to much better use by turning the pages of the book he loved beyond all others, the volume which Jean Jacques Rousseau had devoted to the subject of education?

This ill-assorted couple—the rich and elegant young aristocrat who was very much aware of his good looks and very particular about the cut of his coats, and the slovenly amateur philosopher—should have attracted considerable attention when together they set foot on the soil of their ancestral Spain. But the eighteenth century had been an age of such outspoken "individualism" that a mild eccentric like little Simon Rodriguez passed almost unnoticed and as he traveled in the company of a young gentleman of high social distinction and unlimited credit (for even if Bolivar was of foreign birth, he had almost as many quarterings as the King himself), Rodriguez was received everywhere with that respect and honor which were his due as a true philosopher.

Once in Madrid, Simon Bolivar must soon have noticed that in spite of his being "a colonial," he was all the same a personage of considerable importance. He was presented to both His Majesty the King and to Her Majesty the Queen and he was received with becoming condescension by this couple, who were probably the most unprepossessing occupants of a throne that had never been blessed with an overabundance of either brains or good looks.

Young Bolivar also received a large number of invitations to attend receptions in the most dignified and dullest homes of the Spanish capital, and since all this was new to him, he might even have enjoyed himself in a mild way, except for the fact that he fell hopelessly in love. Now at the age of seventeen, to fall hopelessly in love is tragedy indeed, especially if the father of the object of your affection happens to be the high and mighty Don del Toro, brother of an even higher and mightier Marquis del Toro, whose vast estates in Venezuela make him one of the most influential men in the New World and who (as a neighbor) knows, of course, all about you and your prospects. When in addition we take into consideration the age of the bride (the lovely child had then just turned fifteen), we can understand that the parents of the prospective Señora Bolivar were none too eager to give their consent.

Fortunately, the girl's father was a reasonable gentleman who seems to have been exposed to a few of the new ideas of enlightenment which had so sedulously been banned from Spain. Instead of forbidding the young man his house (the "never darken my door again" attitude so common even in the days of our grandparents) and sending his daughter to a convent (from where she would probably have eloped with the gardener), he invited the young man to his study and in a kindly fashion he told him:

159

"As you, my dear Senor Simon, will see for yourself, you and my daughter are both of you much too young to know your own minds. Marriage is a very solemn business, for marriages are made in heaven. However, I am a man of my own time and age. All I ask of you is to promise me that you will not try to see my daughter for a year and if, at the end of that year, she still wants you for a husband, then we shall meet again and we shall see what we can do about it."

The promise was máde and faithfully kept by both sides. In the year 1801, Simon Bolivar married his beloved Maria Teresa. After that there was nothing to keep him any longer in the Old World and immediately after the wedding, he took his wife to Venezuela. Ten months later, she lay dead, a victim of the annual visitation of yellow fever. And so, at an age when most boys have not even left school, Simon Bolivar found himself a widower, without a home, without a family and with all his high hopes for the future smashed to bits.

To divert the poor youngster, kindhearted Uncle Carlos suggested another trip abroad. Accompanied by his faithful secretary, private-philosopher and tutor, Simon Bolivar once more crossed the ocean and it was on this occasion that that farewell visit to the Vatican took place, during which Simon showed the first signs of that spirit of independence and defiance which was something quite new and entirely unexpected in a young man with his background. This is the way it seems to have come about.

The young Venezuelan, as was his due considering his social standing in the New World, had been granted an audience with the Pope. But when the time came for him to kiss the foot of His Holiness, he deliberately looked the other way and refused to comply with a custom almost as old as the Holy See itself. The excuse he afterwards offered for this serious breach of good form shows that by then he, too, had been most dangerously imbued with the new ideas of self-assertion. He curtly informed the Spanish ambassador, who had taken him to the Vatican, that his respect for the high office of the Pontiff should not be measured by an act of servility.

This was a most unfortunate reply, for it betrayed a sad lack of respect and one might even add good manners. But it was mild, compared to what the soldiers of the Revolution had said and done after they had taken possession of the Patrimony of St. Peter, and since His Holiness, being a wise and understanding man, kindly overlooked this breach of decorum, it was not half as serious in its consequences as that which happened a few days later.

On that morning, the young Don and his faithful shadow, the inevitable Rodriguez, had climbed to the top of that low hill, known as the Mons Sacra, where according to tradition, the common people of Rome in the year 494 B.C. had gathered together to defy the power of the aristocracy. There amidst the ruins of a bygone world, young Simon Bolivar had suddenly seen a great light. He had thrown up both his arms towards heaven and had taken a holy vow that, come what might, he would not allow his hands to be idle nor his soul to rest until he should set his native land free from the yoke of foreign domination.

This story may be true and it may be an invention of later times, after Venezuela had gained its independence. But something of this sort may well have happened, as Bolivar had by then had a chance to observe the greater part of Europe with his own eyes and was not at all pleased at what had presented itself to his gaze. And furthermore, you will find the incident related in all the most reliable biographies of the great Venezuelan.

Quite naturally, after reaching the Old World, Don Simon had first of all gone to Madrid, where perhaps he had hoped to find forgetfulness for the loss of his wife by surrendering himself to such frivolities as the rather dull capital of the Spanish Empire had to offer. But an unfortunate meeting with the royal police had spoiled his taste for the city. He had been taken into custody by the local secret service. He was suspected of being involved in a plot to set Venezuela free. No incriminating documents being found either on his person or among his luggage, he had been set free. The incident, however, had taught him a lesson he was never to forget. If he, once the richest young member of America's colonial society, could be treated like a common criminal, then heaven help the others! And so he had left Madrid, never to see it again.

The story of his wanderings through Europe is complicated and vague, for Bolivar kept no diaries. Rome I have already mentioned. He also visited Venice, as the city of Venice had a special attraction for all good Venezuelans. Did not the very name of Venezuela, or Little Venice, show that their country had first of all been visited by a sailor from the old Venice?

Then Paris had come in for a long stay. At that moment Napoleon was the hero of every up and coming young man in every part of the world. But when Bolivar reached the French capital, the man who had carried the liberal ideas of the French Revolution to every nook and corner of Europe had deliberately betrayed the cause of liberty and equality by proclaiming himself emperor of the French.

That was too much for the pupil of Simon Rodriguez. He refused to attend the coronation ceremonies, for which he had received an invitation. The only other person, by the way, who deliberately stayed away from these festivities was Napoleon's own mother. The old lady was never quite sure where all this glory would lead her son and never ceased to warn him that this foolishness could not possibly last. (It did not.) Bolivar never met Napoleon and it is doubtful whether Napoleon ever heard Bolivar's name until he found himself buried alive on the island of St. Helena. But it was undoubtedly Napoleon's treason to the cause of freedom which cured the young Venezuelan of any desire to tarry longer in the Old World. It had taught him all he cared to learn and, like Jefferson some twenty years earlier, he had come to the conclusion that the Old and the New Worlds had very little in common and that it would be best for each of them to go its own sweet way.

And so after a short walking trip, he took ship for the United States of America, that he might see for himself how fared that interesting new experiment in applied democracy which had been started at about the same time he himself had been born.

He met a few people of note in New York and Philadelphia, but not a great many. In the first place, his knowledge of the English tongue was very scanty and practically no one in the United States knew a word of Spanish. This complete ignorance about the vernacular of the other half of our continent was only equalled (if not actually surpassed) by our lack of information about South America in general. There was no commercial intercourse between these two parts of the world, for the government in Madrid did not allow foreigners to deal with its South American subjects, and culturally, the two Americas were so foreign to each other that when George Tickner of Boston started work on his ponderous *History of Spanish Literature* (published in 1849), he had to send to Europe for a Spanish dictionary as not a single copy was to be found in the United States.

And then there was another reason why these revolutionary movements in the South were regarded with so little sympathy in the North. Immediately after we had gained our independence there had been a great increase in our national wealth. Those whom President Adams described as "the rich, the well-to-do and the able" feared nothing as much as a social upheaval that might increase the power of the common people. And it had been rumored that the different provinces of South America were beginning to be extremely restless under the misrule of their Spanish masters.

Those who considered themselves the most substantial

citizens of the new commonwealth and who were very much afraid that in a true democracy they might lose some of their wealth, seemed to feel that no one else but they themselves had the right to make revolutions. A good many of them were not even so sure that they had done the right thing, when they had got rid of their King. Therefore, young men of South American extraction and with the fire of rebellion in their eyes were not exactly welcome guests in the better-class homes of Philadelphia and Boston. Mr. Jefferson would undoubtedly have liked to meet Don Simon Bolivar and would have done him honor, but there was no one to introduce the two men to each other and the young Venezuelan was allowed to depart as quietly and unobtrusively as he had arrived.

It was a pity but alas, it was entirely in keeping with that harmful lack of vision which during a great many periods of our history has been so characteristic of our dealings with our South American neighbors until the outbreak of the present war. And none of these mistakes was worse than our deliberate neglect of Simon Bolivar during those twenty years of his career when he burned out his life's candle on the steps of the altar of liberty.

Chapter III.

The Beginning of the Battle for Freedom.

WHEN SIMON BOLIVAR, after his many years of wandering and looking, listening and learning, returned to Caracas he was rather pathetically lonesome. He had no definite plans for the future, but that need not have bothered him. He was not obliged to work for a living. He had an income of twenty thousand dollars a year, which was the equivalent of about a hundred thousand dollars today, and he never would have to go hungry. Furthermore, he was a young man without any family obligations, as he never again, after the death of his young wife, showed the slightest desire to contract another marriage.

But it was impossible that anyone with as active a brain as Bolivar should go through life merely playing the rôle of a man about town in a small provincial city in a remote part of the great Spanish Empire of the south. What then was he to do with himself? Politics were out of the question. He could become an officer in the home guard, but that meant nothing more than being allowed to wear a beautiful uniform and dance attendance on the wife of the Spanish Governor whenever her ladyship felt the need of giving a little party and wanted a few extra dancers.

Meanwhile, as Bolivar realized, the world was changing rapidly, even in Venezuela, and he felt convinced that if he only bided his time, something was bound to turn up. It did turn up, but not in the way either he or anybody else had expected.

Up to that time there had been only one and a very badly organized outbreak of discontent on the part of the Venezuelans against the rule of Spain. It had happened in the year 1799, when two patriots had proclaimed a republic. One of them, by the name of España, had been hanged and the other had been condemned to life imprisonment in Spain. After that, peace and quiet had prevailed as before until, quite unexpectedly, something had happened that had completely changed the picture and given the revolutionary elements, both in Spain and in the colonies, their chance.

In the year 1808, weak and flabby King Charles IV of Spain had surrendered his crown to Napoleon and the French Emperor had appointed his own brother, Joseph Bonaparte (the diplomat of the family) as his successor. The Spanish people had angrily refused to accept this former member of the French revolutionary government as their ruler. They would have no dealings with one of these godless cutthroats who had not even hesitated to lay hands on the anointed person of their lord and master.

When Napoleon, in spite of the objections of his newly acquired subjects, had tried to establish Joseph in the royal palace of Madrid, the Spaniards everywhere had risen in open rebellion. Napoleon's representative, General Murat, who stood for no nonsense (having started his own career as part of the revolutionary mob), had ordered the severest kinds of countermeasures and the Spanish patriots had been shot with the same lack of moderation as is shown today towards the unfortunate Norwegians and Dutch who dare to oppose Hitler.

But the very ferocity with which Napoleon had tried to suppress this outbreak of loyalty on the part of the Spanish people had only succeeded in making them more determined than ever not to give in to the usurper, and representatives from every part of the peninsula had come together in Cadiz to proclaim a regency. They had designated Ferdinand, the son of Charles, as the legitimate ruler of Spain and its colonies, and as the representative of his father while the latter was in French custody.

Without realizing it, they had by this entirely legitimate act put certain highly useful cards into the hands of the discontented elements in the colonies. All these honest patriots now had to do to achieve at least a semblance of independence was to declare themselves subjects of their "real King, Ferdinand VII," and to pretend that they were obeying him while they were disobeying his royal papa. For as Ferdinand was in exile (shortly afterwards he, too, was taken prisoner by Napoleon) and could not in any way assert himself, the colonies were for the moment at least being left entirely to their own fate. England could have come to their assistance, but England was much too busy fighting Napoleon in a dozen other parts of the world to bother about such a minor issue as a political upheaval in a little colony somewhere in South America.

Moreover, since the beginning of history, revolutionaries have done their best fishing in troubled waters and never were the political waters of the world more troubled than during the Napoleonic wars. Even the inexperienced leaders from the Venezuela backwoods knew this.

When two representatives of King Joseph made their appearance in La Guaira (the harbor of Caracas, which itself lay safely hidden behind the mountains) and asked the people to swear allegiance to their new king, they had burst forth in great indignation.

"An outrage!" they shouted. "Think of asking loyal Spanish subjects to forswear their real sovereign merely because he cannot send an army to defend them. Perish the idea and *viva el Rey Ferdinando,* who is our real lord and who is upholding the rights of Spain against the French usurper!"

They had created such a commotion that the two Frenchmen had hastily withdrawn to their vessel and had departed for home. Nobody had whispered a word about the possibility of letting Venezuela declare itself independent, but under the circumstances, the results were just about the same, for the Spanish Governor, cut off from his base of supplies, was not in a position to maintain order if anybody should have dared to question his authority.

Alas, there was no one who as yet knew how to question that authority, for the honest young patriots who were trying so desperately to do something for their country were as helpless as babes in the woods when it came to any kind of practical statecraft. They had started their movement for freedom without first finding out for

IN SOUTH AMERICA MOST OF THE FIGHTING WAS DONE IN TERRITORY LIKE THIS

WHILE THIS WAS THE TERRITORY OF THE REVOLUTION IN NORTH AMERICA

Fighting terrain in North and South America.

whom they were speaking and who therefore would be willing to back them up the moment there should be an outbreak of hostilities between themselves and the soldiers of the governor. When that moment arrived (as it was bound to, sooner or later) and they had to face the Spanish mercenaries, they discovered that they stood alone. A handful of young aristocrats were willing to risk everything for the sake of freedom—their lives, their property, the safety of their families! But the small landowners hastily withdrew and so did the tradesmen, the shopkeepers, and all the people who would have benefitted most if the revolution had been successful.

Slavery is almost invariably self-imposed and the common people of Venezuela once again proved the truth of this unhappy saying. They stayed at home and did not move a finger to further the cause of liberty. Just the same, the young patriots went ahead and they were so successful that they actually reached a point where they could issue a declaration of independence for their native land, but the famous *coup d'état* of the nineteenth of April of the year 1810 really accomplished very little, for it had no lasting results. It attracted considerable attention because it was the first document of its kind on the South American continent, but it was like a bonfire on ice. It caused a tremendous flame as long as it actually burned and was seen far and wide, but it did not last very long and as soon as it had been extinguished, the world seemed even darker than before.

True enough, the Spanish Viceroy had been reduced to impotence and a Venezuelan Junta had taken over the reins of government, but everybody knew that this state of affairs could not last unless the revolutionists were able to assure themselves of the support of some foreign government, willing and able to provide them with money and with men.

With this in view, Simon Bolivar, who was known to have had considerable experience with Europe, was chosen to go abroad and try and arouse a little sympathy and support for the cause of Venezuelan liberty. At the same time two other delegates were hopefully despatched to the United States.

Bolivar reached the British capital safely enough but he accomplished very little. The English people accorded him a most cordial reception, for the canny British merchants, foreseeing a fine chance at making a great deal of money from trading with that rich and as yet unexploited continent, were greatly in favor of more and better revolutions in every part of South America.

The Government, however, remained indifferent and it was the attitude of His Majesty and his ministers which mattered. This was rather surprising, for at that very moment a veritable wave of rebellion was sweeping across the whole of the South American continent. In May of the same year, 1810, the Spaniards had been driven out of Buenos Aires. In July they had been forced to give up the city of Bogota. In September, Chile had followed suit and by the end of the year, every important city of the entire continent (with the exception of Lima) had got rid of its Spanish garrison. British commercial interests never ceased bringing this welcome development to the attention of their rulers, but their efforts were a waste of time.

Indeed, it was not until the year 1823 that the British Government finally came to share the views of its rich merchants and then it did not act out of any love for the South Americans but out of fear for the consequences of the so-called Holy Alliance.

This most unholy combination of the reactionary forces of pre-Revolutionary Europe founded in the year 1815 by the Emperors of Russia and Austria and the King of Prussia to keep the world safe for the old reactionary principles, was then taking steps for the re-conquest of the South American continent.

By that time even the United States had recognized the independence of her South American sister-republics, and, fearing that the Holy Alliance might be successful, George Canning, the British foreign minister, had suggested to Washington that a joint note of protest to Ma-

The Spaniards had been driven out of Buenos Aires.

drid against possible foreign interference might not be amiss and would prevent further interference on the part of the big empires of Europe with the affairs of the American continent at large.

The American Government had not been willing to go as far as all that but in his next annual message to Congress, President Monroe laid down the doctrine that from that moment on there must be neither any further colonization nor any more intervention on the part of any European government in so far as the two Americas were concerned.

This warning, by the way, never was ratified by Congress and therefore it never became a formal law for which America might have been asked to fight. It remained merely a "warning," but a "warning" which ever since has been most carefully heeded by the former owners of American colonies.

But here I am again running ahead of my story and I must return to the year 1810, when as yet the British Government had not the slightest inclination towards such a drastic policy as that afterwards laid down in the Monroe Doctrine and when Simon Bolivar was politely informed that he was wasting his time and might just as well go back home.

In his despair, he then decided upon a step which would prove to be so far-reaching that thereafter it would be impossible to continue with the pretense that the Venezuelans' Junta was merely acting as a temporary stopgap for King Ferdinand and that the Venezuelans would return to their former allegiance as soon as His

Majesty should have returned to his palace in Madrid.

What Bolivar did was this. He got in touch with a former fellow countryman who for many years had lived in exile in London and who, some twenty years before, had been forced to flee from South America on account of his revolutionary sentiments. The name of this picturesque figure was Francisco Miranda, who was born in Caracas in the year 1754. In his enthusiasm for the cause of freedom he had hastened to North America to offer his sword to General Washington. Having served with great gallantry in our own Revolutionary Army, he had then made plans for an attack on the Spaniards in his native land, but the plot had been discovered and by way of the United States, Miranda had fled to England.

Having been born with an irrepressible love for adventure, he had next traveled all over Austria and Turkey and had finally reached Russia, where this handsome South American had found such great favor in the eyes of the Empress Catherine that for a while it had actually looked as if, with Russian support, a revolutionary expedition might have actually landed on the shores of our continent. But the Spanish Ambassador in St. Petersburg heard about the plan and through his efforts, the Empress's friend had been forced to leave Russia, and nothing had come of this strange project which might have caused Cossacks to trot through the streets of Caracas.

Miranda had thereupon gone to France, where he had enlisted in the armies of the revolution and had been placed under the command of General Dumouriez. When he had reasons to fear that Dumouriez intended to betray the revolution to the Austrians, he had warned the government in Paris, but this had not prevented him from being arrested any more than did the fact that he had played a leading part in the famous victory of Neerwinden, the first battle, by the way, in which balloons had been used for observation purposes. Acquitted but soon afterwards re-imprisoned, he had only escaped death by the fall of Robespierre and the end of the Reign of Terror.

These harrowing experiences had by no means dampened Miranda's interest in revolutionary activities and as soon as he was back in England, he had once more begun to lay plans for an expedition that should deliver South America from the Spanish yoke. The British Government being uninterested in his plans, he had decided to try his luck in the United States.

There he had met with a reception similar to that in London. Neither President Jefferson nor his Secretary of State, James Madison, would pay attention to Miranda. They had troubles enough of their own, trying to establish some workable and practical kind of democracy on the soil of North America. The only person in Washington who lent a willing (though secret) ear to the widely discussed plans of the conspirator was the Spanish Minister. He hastened to inform his home government to be on the lookout against a surprise attack that might come from the north. So when Miranda had finally persuaded a New York merchant, one Samuel Ogden, to lend him enough money to equip a small expedition and let him try his luck, the soldiers of His Spanish Majesty were waiting

Spanish soldiers were waiting for the little brig.

for him, and when the little brig *Leander*, accompanied by two other vessels, approached the shores of Venezuela in March of the year 1806, the Spaniards for once were ready. Sixty of Miranda's followers were captured. He himself escaped to Trinidad, but ten of his men, eight of them American citizens, were hanged and their heads, cut from their bodies, were shown all over the country as a warning to others who might feel inclined to follow their example and rise against their master, the King.

This time, certain churchmen, too, had been thoroughly alarmed and their parishioners had been warned that this fellow Miranda was a notorious heretic and a dangerous disciple of the revolutionary doctrines of the French Revolution and that he had merely returned to his native land to establish the rule of anti-Christ and to deprive the people not only of their worldly possessions but also of their chance of salvation.

As the British in the West Indies showed no desire whatsoever to give the defeated general the least little bit of support, Miranda had finally returned to London, where he had once more made himself the center of all the plots that were forever being hatched out against the rule of the Spaniards in South America.

Truly a man with his past was not exactly the person to be given a leading role in a movement which still laid pretentions to a certain amount of legitimacy and which claimed that it was only waiting for the happy moment when it could once more place the government in the hands of its beloved ruler, King Ferdinand. Simon Bolivar must have been aware of this when, during his stay in

London, he decided to consult this master mind of the revolutionary technique and suggested that he proceed at once to his native land and take care of the situation.

What made this step all the more dangerous was the fact that in approaching Miranda, Bolivar acted without having consulted his friends at home. They undoubtedly would have advised him against anything quite as drastic, and therefore when the two of them landed in La Guaira in December of the year 1810 they were welcomed with very little enthusiasm. Furthermore, when it was discovered that Miranda, a veteran of many campaigns, was also a strict disciplinarian to whom a revolution was a very serious business, the local patriots, who liked to make speeches and to strut around in their beautiful uniforms, set up a loud hue and cry against this "foreigner" while Miranda's contempt for these "chocolate soldiers" and his general lack of patience with the endless flow of futile oratory soon led to an open break between this self-appointed saviour and those he had come to save.

Bolivar, hopelessly compromised, urged the Junta to have the courage of its convictions, to give up their silly pretense that they were merely acting as the representatives of some distant king, and boldly to declare themselves independent, as the people of North America had done a generation before. The Junta agreed with him but, just the same, it continued to talk and to debate. At last, however, it was persuaded to show a feeble sign of courage, at the insistent urging of Bolivar, and on July fourth of the year 1811 (just thirty-five years after our own Dec-

179

laration of Independence) the leaders of Venezuela declared themselves independent and suggested to the rest of the people of South America that they do likewise and join in a new nation to be known as the Republic of Columbia.

Although Bolivar had been very effective in bringing about this happy solution, the Declaration of Venezuelan Independence did not bear his signature. He had not been considered of sufficient importance to be allowed to share in this great honor and he had to content himself with the not very flattering role of being a mere spectator in the acting out of the great drama, whereas he had been one of the main actors.

But perhaps it was just as well that he did not play too conspicuous a role at that particular time, for this noble document, alas, was not destined to have a very long existence. The first Venezuelan revolution was a complete failure and came to a very sad end. It was the old story of a people who were completely lacking in training in the difficult business of "practical politics" and who were unable to sacrifice their personal ambitions for a common purpose.

Even Miranda and Bolivar were unable to work together harmoniously and the only condition on which Miranda was willing to assume the commandership-in-chief of all the revolutionary armies was that Bolivar should be excluded from taking part in the forthcoming campaign. With a fine flourish of his sword, Bolivar thereupon offered to go as a common soldier, but his late wife's uncle, the Marquis del Toro, took him on his staff, so the man who had inspired the revolt was finally permitted to take an active part in the fighting in the role of an officer.

Then there arose new difficulties. The constitution which the Junta had finally adopted placed all power in the hands of three men, but Bolivar, who knew his fellow countrymen, was in favor of a strong one-man executive and declared that the arrangement of triumvirate (as history had amply shown) could never lead to anything but chaos.

After that, the fat was in the fire. Everybody talked and talked at once and nobody did anything. The Spaniards, making good use of this welcome opportunity, badly defeated the noble Marquis del Toro.

Meanwhile, all those elements of the population (and they were still considerable) which detested the principles of the French Revolution and feared the worst if they should fall a prey to the wild men of Caracas, were beginning to turn their backs upon those who were fighting for their freedom. Indeed, the country was on the brink of civil war and further removed from freedom than ever before. Then Nature took a hand and completely undid everything the patriots had so far accomplished.

On Holy Thursday of the year during which these momentous events took place, just when the people of Caracas had gathered together in their churches, the town was shaken by the worst earthquake that part of the world had ever experienced. Twelve thousand people were killed. The number of those wounded and maimed was never revealed, but the disaster was so terrific that it threw the populace into a state of abject panic.

It was an ideal moment for the Church to reassert its power. With quite a few notable exceptions, priests, monks, and nuns had been on the side of the monarchy. They might have certain very definite grievances of their own against too much meddling on the part of Madrid with purely clerical affairs, but with even greater anxiety they had watched the steady growth of the hated revolutionary ideas. Now the conservative element had their chance. No sooner had the earth ceased to tremble than they were explaining how this calamity was really an act of God, who had used this method to show His displeasure. Let the people of Caracas take warning and turn out the scoundrels who had intended to lead them down the pathway to perdition.

The illiterate masses, left for centuries without so much as a single public school and hopelessly bewildered by their misfortunes, listened only too eagerly. When a short time later, Spanish reinforcements arrived in La Guaira, they found the road to Caracas wide open. Miranda made ready to defend himself but he was betrayed by one of his own officers and was forced to sue for an armistice. At the end of the armistice, the Spanish commander promised that Miranda and all his men would be allowed to leave in peace.

What happened after that has ever remained a mystery. There was a lot of loose talk that Miranda had sold out to the Spaniards, but subsequent events hardly justify such an unpleasant suspicion, for Miranda, just when he was ready to board ship for Europe, was taken prisoner by orders of the Spanish commander. Eventually he was transferred to Spain, where in a dark cell he was chained to the wall like a wild animal. He never again saw the light of day. In the year 1816, death put an end to his miseries. That was the terrible fate of a man who, in spite of his many shortcomings, will ever remain one of the most colorful figures of the great South American struggle for liberty.

As for Bolivar, just before the earthquake he had again had words with Miranda, who had thereupon sent him to the distant city of Puerto Cabello, the harbor of Valencia, there to await his further instructions, which of course never came.

After the surrender of Miranda, Bolivar realized not only that the cause of independence had been lost for a long time to come but also that his name must be mentioned quite prominently on the lists of those whom the Spanish Government eventually meant to execute. There was nothing left for him but flight. He took a vessel and sailed for the Dutch island of Curaçao, there to await the coming of a new and happier day.

Thus the curtain descended upon the first act of Simon Bolivar's career as the saviour of his native land. It was true that he had not exactly covered himself with glory in action and that in the end he had even been hooted off the scene. But he was still very young and still full of hope and energy, although his estates had been confiscated by the Spaniards and he was completely penniless. His name, however, was still good for a considerable amount of credit, at least among the moneylenders of the Caribbean.

When Bolivar heard that there still were faint stirrings of rebellion in the western part of New Granada, he decided to make common cause with the small group of insurgents which continued to operate in the vicinity of Cartagena. He borrowed a few hundred dollars and in the year 1812, the year of Napoleon's disastrous campaign in Russia, he once more set foot on the soil of his native land. That was the beginning of the second act of the great drama that was to be forever associated with his name.

Chapter IV.

Days of Glory.

BOLIVAR LIVED all his life surrounded by a heavy spray of ink. He must have been the best customer the manufacturers of goose quill pens ever had, for no sooner had he settled down for a few moments of rest and relaxation than he would think of something he must at once communicate to his fellow men and he was busy instantly writing still another document of state.

That all these high-sounding *pronunciamentos* to the world at large were of equal importance, I would hardly dare to assert. Some of them are painfully bombastic, at least to our ears, but we must not forget that in such matters (as in several others) the tastes of the Spaniards are apt to be somewhat different from our own. And a hundred and fifty years ago, our own domestic politicians could also make the eagle scream with scant respect for the rules and regulations which Marcus Tullius Cicero had so eloquently laid down for the guidance of his brethren of the oratorical fraternity. But, like all people who either write or speak a lot, Bolivar would have his happy moments and then he was more than good—then he was really excellent.

The appeal he addressed to the people of New Granada

shortly after his arrival in Cartagena belongs to his more fortunate expressions of opinion upon the subject of state-craft and as such it deserves our very serious attention. The document is dated December 15, 1812, and in a way it resembles that other great last will and testament, Washington's Farewell Address, except that it was written at the beginning of our hero's active career and not at the end. It reveals the wide gap that existed between our own ideals about liberty and self-government and those that were to prevail for such a long period of time in the southern half of our common continent.

We should, of course, also remember that Bolivar was still deeply disheartened and depressed by the dreadful failure of his people's first attempt to establish themselves as an independent nation. He reasserts his absolute belief in the rights of man and in the sovereignty of the people at large. But before these natural privileges can be exercised, so he argues, it is necessary that a nation shall have achieved something more than an independence that exists only on paper. And face to fact with a cruel and relentless enemy (the Spanish monarchy), a revolution must learn to be just as hard as its opponents and must not lose itself in too much theorizing.

Words are powerless against bullets, and an army composed only of generals but without any soldiers will probably never be very successful when it finds itself opposed by the trained hirelings of a foreign despot. "Therefore, oh unfortunate people of Venezuela," he pleaded, "repent of your past mistakes and first of all learn to obey. Do not forever grant pardons to those who have betrayed the holy cause of freedom, but destroy them as an example to those others who might feel inclined to do likewise because they know that should they be captured, they will suffer no worse fate than a few years of exile. South America should belong to the South Americans. The wicked foreign oppressors should be driven from every nook and corner of the whole of the continent, but this glorious end can only be accomplished if the people of South America will learn to forget a few of their personal rights and will accept the dictates of those whom they have chosen to be their leaders."

To be quite honest about it, there was nothing very new in this line of reasoning. The Greeks had listened to similar harangues when their freedom was threatened by the grasping ambitions of their Macedonian neighbors. All through history, we have had plentiful examples of what will happen to those who have put the cart before the horse and who demand the sweet fruits of liberty before that liberty has actually been gained.

"A government," to quote from Bolivar's Cartagena Manifesto, "must adapt itself to the times and the circumstances under which it lives. If the times happen to be prosperous and if everything is serene, a government can afford to be lenient and easygoing, but if the times are dangerous, a government must know how to inspire terror and fear. And it must arm itself with that firmness which is required by the dangers which menace the safety of the land, without a thought for either law or constitution, and it must continue to do so until peace and prosperity shall have been brought about. If the people of Venezuela had established a simple and workable form of government, such as was required by the political and military situation, then they would still enjoy their recently won liberty, whereas now they are once more slaves at the mercy of a foreign master."

Looked at from the point of view of the year 1812, the document made sense. It is very easy for us to denounce it as an appeal to dictatorship, but our own history has only too clearly shown that during an emergency there has got to be a single head or all will be lost. We happen to have been very fortunate in the choice of our great leaders. George Washington and Abraham Lincoln were able to exercise dictatorial power without evincing the slightest desire to set themselves up as tyrants. They took hold of a desperate situation, they solved it and quietly returned to the ranks of common citizens.

In South America on the other hand, such "emergency leaders" have been only too apt to want the job for life, but in his main contentions, Bolivar was right. A revolution can never hope to succeed unless it adopt the methods of a victorious army, and no army will ever gain a victory if every private has the right to question his officers' decisions and is allowed to act as he pleases while under fire or in the line of march.

Bolivar's enemies, of course, explained his observations as a bid on his part for a dictatorship. They knew him to be a young man of unlimited ambition and they realized how hard it must have been for him to find himself pushed back into a minor position, while other men of much smaller calibre were taking charge of affairs. I can't quite agree with this point of view. The proof of the pudding is in the eating and when it came to eating the pudding, Simon Bolivar was always extremely careful to avoid even the appearance of aspiring to any higher rank than that of being known as the Liberator.

By instinct and due to his original surroundings, he was an aristocrat. That is to say, he cared only for what was best in life and accepted no compromise with the second-best. But at the same time, he believed sincerely in the new principles of liberty and fraternity and equality. Not in that sentimental way of which we see so many evidences around us today, when statesmen are forever glorifying the virtues of the "plain people." The plain people, as Bolivar was clever enough to understand, are neither better nor worse than the non-plain people and unless they make up their minds to accept a certain amount of discipline, they will never get anywhere at all.

That—as far as I see it—is what Bolivar meant to say in his famous Cartagena letter, and having had his say, he dropped his goose quill and once more reached for his sword. This time, however, he did not have to content himself with a minor position somewhere behind the fighting front, for the year 1812, which witnessed the fall of Napoleon, also saw the rise of Bolivar as a military leader.

The next pages of this story will therefore be full of war and the clamor of war. I shall try and make it as brief as possible but that will not be easy, for the territory to be covered will be very large. Moreover, we are apt to be really rather inexcusably ignorant about the history of

South America. That makes us forget that the military activities of Bolivar lasted three times as long as those of George Washington; that the territory he and San Martin covered was almost fifty times as large as the territory covered by our own Revolutionary Armies (reaching all the way from the Plate River to the Isthmus of Panama); and that whereas our soldiers experienced only one winter of Valley Forge, the followers of Bolivar never got far beyond the confines of such a hunger-camp but remained faithful to their leader for almost twenty years.

Bolivar had now learned a few highly useful lessons about the way his campaign must be fought. War, he had come to understand, was a grim business and he was dealing with an enemy as perfidious and as willing to break its word as any other of which history has kept the record and that record is a long and sad one. It was useless to be polite and it was fatal to show mercy when he knew that, in case of defeat, no clemency whatsoever would be shown to the captured revolutionaries. He therefore invented a new slogan: "War to the death to all Spaniards!" And at the same time, he appealed to all South Americans to make common cause with their brethren of Venezuela. For Bolivar, although then only at the beginning of his career, was already thinking in "continental terms," rather than in merely "provincial terms," beyond which most of his contemporaries could never lift themselves.

It was he—Simon Bolivar—who soon afterwards was to make the first suggestion about a United States of the whole American continent. The idea was still rather vague. He had not yet devoted any attention to the details connected with such a vast scheme. But he was the first man to think of such a possibility and he should be given full credit.

Since such a United American Continent would not be possible until first of all the last of the foreign soldiers should have been driven from American soil, he lashed forth against them in his appeal for a war without mercy. His bitter denunciation was not received with general approval. On the contrary, his violent words shocked a great many people. They sounded too bloodthirsty. But after the war had been going on for only a few years and the Spaniards had shown what they could and would do whenever any revolutionary soldiers or civilians fell into their hands, it was proven by dozens of outrageous massacres that he had been very wise in choosing his slogan.

And then—for a short while at least—the war for freedom became a struggle of life or death. There were no "honorable surrenders," as were so common in our own revolution. You either killed your enemy or he killed you. You either hanged him or he hanged you. There were no longer any compromises or halfway measures.

On this occasion Bolivar started his campaign of revolution by a sudden thrust which opened up the valley of the Magdalena River to the forces of the rebellion. After that had been done, he turned eastward at the head of an army (if such it could be called) of fewer than eight hundred men. They were so flushed with victory that they easily defeated fifteen thousand Spanish royalist troops which had been sent to intercept them and prevent them from reaching Caracas.

After the battles of Merida and Trujillo, the road to the Venezuelan capital stood wide open and on August 6th, 1813, Bolivar marched into Caracas, after a campaign of only ninety days, during which time he had covered a distance of some 750 miles, had fought six pitched battles and had destroyed five royalist armies, which had fled with a loss of fifty cannon.

There was a reason for this sudden change in his fortunes. During the period that lay between the first Venezuelan revolt and the campaign of the year 1813, the Spanish authorities had made themselves so thoroughly unpopular that this time the revolutionary soldiers were welcomed as real deliverers. Bolivar himself was offered any position he might wish to accept; but with his conspicuous gift for the right word at the right moment, he answered that the only office he would accept was that of a plain soldier forever in the post of danger at the head of his "comrades." He would allow the people to call him their Liberator but beyond that humble appellation, he had no ambitions.

And he proved himself as good as his word when on December fifth of the same year, 1813, he assumed command of the revolutionary army and so thoroughly trounced a royalist army of 3500 men that he put an end to all further opposition on the part of the Spanish colonial authorities. This time it looked as if Venezuela had at last gained its freedom, and it would have done so if the Spaniards had not found an unexpected ally among the cowboys who roamed the *llanos,* those vast plains that lay due west of the Orinoco River and that were not unlike the pampas of the Argentine.

The history of South America, by and large, is a long, sanguinary one, but the honor of having been the most degraded and contemptible figure among all those who had played a role in the events of those days goes undoubtedly to the leader of those *llaneros* who fought for plunder and for the joy of bloodshed.

The man who then appeared upon the scene called himself José Tomas Boves, though that may not have been the real name of this red-haired monster. Of one thing we are sure, he was not an American. He was a full-blooded Spaniard, from the province of Asturias in the old country. He had started his career as a pirate in the Caribbean and after his capture by the Spaniards, he had spent a long time in jail. From Puerto Cabello, where he had been imprisoned, he had somehow found his way to the *llanos* and, being a born leader, he had had no difficulty in organizing the half-civilized horsemen of that region into a first-rate and well-disciplined gangster army.

In his first encounter with this dangerous new enemy, Bolivar was successful. On February 12th, 1814, near La Victoria, his men, carefully entrenched according to the best rules of war, caused terrific havoc among the cowboy cavalry of Boves. But when they followed up their victory by a pursuit of the rapidly retreating horsemen, they came upon a dreadful scene of carnage. Whole villages had been wiped out, and their inhabitants, men and women and children, had been slain or mutilated. This drove the men who fought for freedom into such an outbreak of rage that even Bolivar, who until then had always been quite generous in the treatment of his prisoners of war, lost patience and ordered the execution of some nine hundred of Boves' men.

If Bolivar had hoped that this merciless slaughter would teach the *llaneros* a lesson, he was mistaken. When in June of the year 1814, in the first battle of La Puerta, Boves defeated the troops of Bolivar and returned to Caracas, he killed more than 3500 refugees who had fled to the capital in the hope of reaching La Guaira and escaping by way of the sea.

Bolivar himself eluded the fate that awaited so many of his fellow men, but only by a stroke of luck and just when he was on the point of being captured. With the unreasoning anger of panic-stricken men, many of his officers thereupon denounced him as a traitor and accused him of having deliberately delivered his army into the hands of the *llaneros*. Fortunately, in Cartagena the Congress which held his fate in its hands remembered his former victories rather than his single defeat and it felt such confidence in his military abilities that it gave him command of the troops, which meanwhile had been gathered together to march against the city of Bogota, the biggest and most dangerous stronghold that still held out and flew the flag of Spain.

On this occasion General Chance fought on Bolivar's side, but immediately afterwards he returned to the camp of the Liberator's enemies and in the battle of Santa Marta the rebels were so badly defeated that they lost over a thousand men and more than a hundred cannon.

And what was the cause of this unfortunate disaster? The same old story of jealousy and lack of loyalty. A dozen other men had wanted to be in charge of the army. Envious of the ever increasing prestige of Bolivar, they had done everything within their power to prevent him from gaining a victory. Deeply outraged by this manifestation of ingratitude and by the cowardly conduct of many of his subordinates, Bolivar was ready to give up. He swore that he would never again move a finger on behalf of a people who were born to be slaves. And being as good as his word, he sailed for the British island of Jamaica, with the intention of going back to Europe and withdrawing for good and all from American politics.

As usual, Simon Bolivar's mood of despair was short-lived. The cause of freedom was too close to his heart that he could have spent the rest of his days as a private citizen in some little English or French town. He had never been the man to take his responsibilities lightly. Every day brought him fresh stories of the outrages being committed by the victorious Spaniards. Hundreds of patriots were shot. Others were hanged. Many more were disappearing in those dungeons of the fortresses along the coast from which no one had ever been known to return alive.

Even Bolivar himself, although living on neutral soil, was no longer safe. One night, tired out by his efforts to raise enough money for still another expedition, he decided to take a walk. When he returned to his lodgings, he found that a friend of his had used his absence to snatch a few moments' rest, and had stretched himself out on Bolivar's couch. When Bolivar shook him, he found that his friend was dead. A former slave of the Liberator had stuck a knife into the sleeper's back and had killed him.

The British authorities, who have never looked with favor on political assassination, quickly caught the murderer and had him executed. At the same time, fearing a repetition of that sort of thing, they gave a hint to Bolivar that his absence would be much more welcome than his presence. They knew, of course, that he was getting ready for another invasion of his native land and they did not wish to be mixed up in any further revolutionary activities. They had just rid themselves of their old enemy, the great Napoleon. It had taken them almost twenty years to do the job. For the moment, all they wanted was peace and quiet and a chance to recuperate from a generation of uninterrupted warfare.

In Spain, King Ferdinand had meanwhile succeeded his father, King Charles, and Spain was once more able to handle its own affairs. Unfortunately, the new ruler proved to be quite as bad as his predecessor. He was a perfect Bourbon in his complete inability to learn from experience. No sooner had he been firmly re-established in Madrid than he had revoked the few wise measures which the faithful Junta in Caracas had passed while acting as his nominal representatives during the period when he had been an exile. Considering himself responsible to no one but to the God who had so kindly recalled him to the throne of his ancestors, he ruled his realm with

It was a land dominated by fortresses and violence.

the ferocious cruelty of a madman. His main ambition seems to have been to get even with those who had been bold enough to defy his authority. Simon Bolivar was his pet abomination and the instructions His Majesty gave to the general in command of the fleet that was to reconquer South America do not make pleasant reading. They become positively painful when we remember that General Morillo, who was at the head of this squadron (the largest naval force equipped by Spain since the days of the Invincible Armada of the year 1588), had been chosen for the job at the suggestion of the great Duke of Wellington. His Grace was undoubtedly a very fine soldier but he did not take any stock in the revolutionary nonsense that was still being practiced in so many parts of the world. He felt that the sooner these detestable doctrines were wiped out, the better it would be for everybody concerned.

Most magnificently did Don Pablo Morillo live up to the high expectations his royal master and his British friend and supporter had placed in him. Day after day the list of proscripts grew smaller as larger and larger numbers of patriots were being killed by the royal Spanish shooting squads and every island of the Caribbean was rapidly being filled by shiploads of fugitives who had escaped with their lives but with the loss of everything they had ever called their own.

As for Bolivar, he was now scot-free but a liberal reward awaited the murderer who would rid His Majesty from this bothersome enemy. He was, however, more than usually careful and spent his time inside the house of a friend, writing manifestoes and trying to raise enough money for still another expeditionary force.

Generally speaking, the tone of his Jamaica *pronunciamentos* remained very much the same as that which people remembered from his famous Cartagena declaration of the year 1812.

In one private letter to a British merchant of Kingston (the capital of Jamaica) he once again expressed his opinions upon the situation in so clear a fashion that I feel inclined to repeat at least part of it. These few lines will show that adversity had by no means broken Simon Bolivar's old fighting spirit and that he was still of the same opinion in regard to the real reason for this latest disaster as he had been after his first defeat.

"Suddenly and without any previous practice or experience in public affairs," so he wrote to his friend, Maxwell Hyslop, "we were forced to assume the responsibilities of running an organized state. We had had no opportunity to develop the talents and public virtues of our brethren of the United States and since we have not yet attained any of those qualities, we cannot yet accept their system. As a result, for the time being we cannot be a true republic. We still need the care of a paternal form of government by which to heal the wounds of despotism and war. In short, we do not of course want a monarchy but at the same time, we are not yet fit for a truly republican form of government. So let us seek a mean between these two extremes. Let us leave the ideal for the future while at the present time we occupy ourselves with whatever is practical for us here and now."

Wise words but at that moment not exactly expressing the sentiments of His Majesty's government in London, which was then following a policy of "Peace at any Price." But let it be added, to the everlasting credit of the non-official English, that they by no means shared the reactionary views of their King and his ministers.

Several private citizens of Trinidad, among them a Jewish merchant by the name of Luis Brion, not only offered Bolivar the use of their ships but were also willing to risk a few thousand dollars of their own on a new venture to drive the Spaniards from the soil of the South American continent. On a gossipy little island like Trinidad, such goings on could not remain a secret for very long and for a second time Bolivar received an official command to leave his place of exile within twenty-four hours and please try his luck somewhere else. And then (as was so often the case during his career), the unexpected happened, out of a clear sky. Bolivar received an invitation from the president of the sovereign republic of Haiti, who wrote that he would consider it an honor if the distinguished Señor Bolivar would come to him as his guest and would stay as long as he liked. Simon Bolivar was deeply grateful and, without any delay, he accepted the invitation and sailed for Port au Prince.

Here once more we must pause for a moment of reflection. In the United States, not a finger was moved to help the Liberator in his efforts to establish freedom among the people of South America, whereas one Alexander Petion, a black man and a former slave, went very far out of his way to favor that same cause of liberty. Not only did he welcome all other fugitives from Spanish persecution, but he also housed them and fed them the same rations his own soldiers received. And when Bolivar set foot on the soil of Haiti, he was greeted with royal honors and was immediately provided with the funds he needed to equip his third (or was it his fourth?) expeditionary corps.

Haiti was a very poor country, but it did the best it could. The force at Bolivar's command, when in November of the year 1815 he set sail for the coast of New Grenada, consisted of 250 men. Louis Brion, his friend from Jamaica, acted as admiral of the ships that were to take part in this mad venture. There were enough supplies to keep both sailors and soldiers from starving for three weeks.

The first thing Bolivar did after he reached the mainland was to proclaim the freedom of all slaves. This bold and unprecedented step was undoubtedly the result of a promise which Bolivar had made to his benefactor just before he sailed. Quite naturally, President Petion of Haiti wanted to do something for his own people and it was only reasonable that he should have asked for some "small favor" in return for the benefits he had showered upon his recent guest. It is interesting to reflect that Bolivar issued his Proclamation of Emancipation exactly forty-seven years before President Lincoln did likewise in our own country.

Having thus incidentally gained the good will of all black Venezuelans, Bolivar began his march in the general direction of Cartagena. Realizing that the forces at his command were too weak to be effective, he hastened back to Haiti to ask for further assistance and once more Petion rose to the occasion. With fresh troops at his disposal, Bolivar (most ably assisted by his beloved friend, Antonio José Sucre) now started boldly against the enemy.

The capture of the city of Angostura on the Orinoco River gave him command of the hinterland. Then General Chance (always a most restless kind of person) must have remembered that he had not treated the Liberator any too generously during their last encounter and decided to help him out.

In a skirmish not long before, a Venezuelan soldier (a mere boy who hardly knew what he was doing) had succeeded in killing the unspeakable Boves. The *llaneros* had been obliged to choose a new leader. And the man they had selected as Boves' successor had been a very different kind of person. Instead of hating all Venezuelans, he loved them so well that he never would do a thing for anybody else. His name was José Antonio Paez and, like Boves, he was a simple, illiterate cowboy, without any kind of education. But he happened to have been born on South American soil and he hated all Spaniards as cordially as Boves had loved them. Paez therefore hastened to join the side of the Liberator. So the *llaneros*, willing to follow any man in whom they recognized the qualities of true leadership and without any deep political convictions of their own, now fought on the side of freedom with the same reckless bravery with which they had previously supported the cause of tyranny.

When Bolivar, setting aside all pretense at being a "dandified, big-city man," actually joined the *llaneros* and lived the rough life of the open fields, their enthusiasm knew no bounds. Together they defeated the Spaniards so completely that Angostura could now be made the capital of the newly established revolutionary confederacy and everything seemed so bright and promising that a beginning was made towards the setting up of a regular civil government.

But General Chance, fickle and undependable as ever, had already tired of his decision to fight on the side of the patriots. Once more he hastened over to the camp of the royalists and in the third battle of La Puerta, on March fifteenth of the year 1818, General Morillo's forces not only defeated those of Simon Bolivar but the Liberator himself was severely wounded and only escaped capture by galloping away on his horse and finding a refuge in the house of a peasant.

The rout of the revolutionary forces had been so complete that the cause of South American freedom seemed lost for good and all. And it would have been, except for that streak of tenacity and obstinacy in Bolivar's character which, in this respect at least, made him a faithful counterpart of our own General Washington, who was never more resourceful than immediately after he had suffered still another setback.

The moment Bolivar was again able to handle a pen, he sat at his little improvised desk and continued the war by means of his endless paper messages. To the authorities of New Grenada (now without any authority, but holding on, nevertheless) he promised that soon all of Venezuela would arise and come to their assistance. He delighted the Angosturians with his visions of a speedy victory, in which case they would have the honor of being the first to proclaim the unity of the whole of South America, and to anybody who wanted anything, he was willing to give double of what they asked.

In the meantime, he was rapidly regaining his health. He thereupon showed that some time during his busy life he must have been able to make a careful study of the campaigns of Hannibal, Caesar, and Napoleon, for in the year 1819 Bolivar established a reputation for himself as one of the greatest experts of all time in what today is known as a *blitzkrieg*.

Thus far he had invariably attacked the Spaniards from the sea side and from the north. This time he decided to surprise them from the rear and so, early in the month of May of the year 1819, at the head of only 2500 men and with hardly any artillery at all, he lost himself among the mountains.

By and large, this trip across the Andes was quite as difficult as that undertaken twenty centuries before by Hannibal, when he decided to cross the Alps, for Hannibal followed a pass that had been known since prehistoric times, whereas Bolivar had to cross the Andes at a spot where there were no roads of any kind. Furthermore, Bolivar's men were badly provided with clothes and most of them had no shoes. During the day, the full heat of a blazing sun descended upon them, while at night the temperature went way down to the freezing point. Then

The soldiers of Bolivar crossed the Andes.

there was that terrible wind, which was a mixture of cold air shot through with rain and snow and sleet. To make matters worse, before Bolivar's followers had reached the foothills of the Andes, they had been obliged to cross the swampy region of the Orinoco, and before they had had an opportunity to dry their clothes and weapons, they had found themselves among the snow fields of the mountains.

When, after endless hardships, they finally reached the plains of New Granada, they were met with the disheartening news that, in spite of all their efforts at secrecy, the Spanish Governor had somehow got wind of their venture and had collected not less than five thousand men with whom to meet their own exhausted forces of only half that number.

Bolivar had only a few days in which to prepare for the battle, which he knew to be unavoidable, but he used this short interval to such good purpose that when the clash occurred, he practically annihilated the forces of the king and took more than two thousand prisoners. Those who survived escaped to the city of Bogota, where they were soon afterwards joined by the Spanish viceroy and his court. This battle, by the way, is known in South America as the battle of the bridge of Boyaca and we have nothing quite to compare with it in our own history except the surrender of Cornwallis which put an end to our Revolution.

A few days afterwards, the soldiers of Bolivar, dirty and exhausted by their long marches through the jungle and across the mountains but full of courage and hope for the future, entered the city of Bogota. Simon Bolivar became the hero of the hour but as on all former occasions, when he could have had any office he wanted, he declined all official honors, although he agreed to accept the title of Liberator of New Granada, as he had already accepted that of Liberator of Venezuela.

Everything seemed set for the final victory, but no sooner had the flowers and the confetti been removed from the streets of Bogota than there was a recurrence of those difficulties which twice before had spoiled everything just when independence seemed to have been established on a permanent basis. Human nature is undoubtedly capable of great changes but it takes a lot of time to bring them about—and even more patience than time—and then it is still mostly a matter of luck.

One of Bolivar's best generals happened to be a native Columbian, a certain Francisco de Paula Santander. He was a first-rate fighter but in more than one sense of the word, as he was of a highly suspicious character and was forever quarreling with both his enemies and his friends. In spite of Bolivar's warning that all the Spanish captives must this time be treated in a humane way, Santander suddenly ordered that thirty-nine Spanish officials who had surrendered to him be shot and be shot in the back, like common criminals. When Bolivar reproved him for this act of wanton cruelty, he excused himself by saying that the feelings of the people of Bogota had been so wrought up by the atrocities committed by Morillo's armies that had he done otherwise, there would have been riots and lynchings.

207

Unfortunately, Bolivar badly needed Santander, for he was a local hero with a loyal local following and so he allowed the matter to drop. But relations between the two men remained strained and in the end, they led up to that plot by which Santander, several years later, tried to murder his rival.

For the moment, however, the two men maintained an outer semblance of mutual respect. Leaving Santander in charge, Bolivar returned to Venezuela to work for his pet plan, the formation of one large republic that should include all the different provinces of the northern part of South America.

He found conditions in Venezuela better than he dared to hope for and the Venezuelan Congress was for once willing to listen to his plans. The republic—his republic—that dream for which he had worked so many years and in spite of so many defeats and disappointments—had at last become a reality.

It was called the Republic of Greater Colombia and it consisted of the present-day sovereign states of Venezuela, Colombia, and Ecuador, which was then known as Quito after its capital city. Simon Bolivar himself was acclaimed as the first president of this republic. He was then in his thirty-sixth year.

Bolivar still had a few more years to live but they were to be a period of almost constant defeat and disappointment. Let it be said to his everlasting credit that during this final chapter, he showed himself an even greater man than he had been when he had the world at his feet and was acclaimed as South America's foremost citizen.

Chapter V.

The Perils of Peace.

THE POWER OF Spain had been broken but the danger was not yet over, for Spain might decide to make a final effort and the Union of Greater Colombia, exhausted by years of civil and foreign war, was in no condition to defend itself adequately in still another struggle. A period of peace was badly needed and though Bolivar himself would have preferred to continue the war, now that he had the Spaniards on the run in every part of his domains, both prudence and wisdom told him to proceed carefully and to desist, for the moment at least, from trying to unite the whole of South America into one vast and unified nation. After a short period of negotiations, he concluded an armistice with the Spanish authorities and thus was able to devote all his energies towards the difficult task of civil reconstruction.

One good thing at least was to come out of this truce. Both parties agreed that henceforth they would behave like civilized human beings and that, should there be a continuation of the fighting, they would respect the rights of all non-belligerents and would refrain from confiscating private property.

They soon had a chance to find out how far they could

or would stick to these high-sounding promises, for when there was a fight in the streets of Maracaibo (still in Spanish hands), the Spanish Governor accused Bolivar of having broken the stipulations of the armistice and he insisted that a state of war once more existed between the republicans and the monarchists. Bolivar suggested that the Maracaibo incident be submitted to arbitration but the Spaniard refused to consider such a reasonable solution. It would have been better had he shown a slightly more conciliatory attitude, for on June 24th of the year 1821, in the battle of Carabobo, the troops of King Ferdinand were so overwhelmingly defeated that their cause was now definitely lost.

Bolivar was naturally delighted with this immediate result but he had grave misgivings about the future. He could handle his people during times of stress, when they needed him to protect their common country against the armies of the Spanish crown, but what would they do, now that peace was within reach? For the moment they no longer had to fear foreign intervention, so all the old local and provincial quarrels would probably break loose and this time with renewed force. Every little policaster would loudly proclaim that it was he, and he alone, who had saved the nation and was therefore entitled to all the rewards. There would be outbreaks of civilians and the prejudices born out of centuries of living in remote little villages and inaccessible valleys would reassert themselves. San Cristobal would insist that it had made greater sacrifices than Merida, and Bogota would insist that its men were braver and its women more beautiful than those of Caracas.

In the end, Bolivar felt so uncertain about the future that he went to the extreme of tendering his resignation as president of the newly formed republic. He knew only too well how many enemies he had made for himself by his many years of success and how his so-called collaborators were only too apt to point at him and then ask each other, "Will you please tell me what he has got that we have not?"

During the last fifteen years of his life, Bolivar had almost continually been either in the field fighting his endless campaign or wandering across the surface of this earth as a fugitive with a price on his head. During this period he had fallen in love with quite a number of women but he had never had the time to marry one of them and to establish some kind of a home for himself. He always seems to have had a premonition that he would not reach a very great age. Those of his relatives who had not been killed during the revolutionary wars had died rather early of the family ailment—weak lungs and a tendency towards tuberculosis.

Yes, Bolivar told himself, the time had come to withdraw completely from active life. But circumstances would not allow this. There still was so much to be done and who could handle all the difficulties that presented themselves almost hourly better than the man who had been on the inside of everything that had been done during the last fifteen years? And so he continued to act as President of the Republic of Greater Colombia and to devote all his energy towards the pretty hopeless purpose

211

of establishing a form of government that would be a great deal less complicated and a great deal better suited to maintain itself against its enemies, both from the outside and from the inside, than the one he had to deal with at the time.

Being a man of action rather than talk (although on occasions he knew how to indulge in a very effective form of rhetoric) he could never overcome his dislike of politics and he was soon busy again with his pet project—the plan for a united South America as a beginning for a union of all American nations. Past experience had taught him not to have any hopes of help from the United States of America, which continued in its former indifference about the nations of the southern half of the continent, so he concentrated upon gaining the goodwill of the people a little nearer by. As a first step in the right direction, he promised his immediate neighbors that should they wish to join his union, they would be permitted to retain their former boundaries and a maximum of local sovereignty.

Now for what is to follow immediately afterwards, I must ask you to let me make another slight detour. Otherwise, the subsequent adventures of Bolivar would make very little sense. We should remember that Bolivar did not operate in a vacuum. There was a lot more to South America than that northern part in which he had thus far operated. Just as important events had taken place in the southern half of the continent as in the northern, and other leaders, just as brave and just as resourceful as himself, had been fighting valiantly in the cause of freedom.

Due to our general indifference about South America,

even the names of their greatest men have meant nothing to quite a few of us. How many of us, for example, have ever heard the name of San Martin, unless we may have visited in Buenos Aires? I have made some experiments along this line and I have come to very disheartening results. San Martin was in every respect as important a personage as George Washington, but few North Americans seemed to know who he was. Here is his story.

José de San Martin was born in the year 1778 in the little village of Yapeyu, situated on the river Uruguay, a part of the world which today belongs to the Republic of Argentine. At an early age he had been sent to Spain to be trained for military service at the Royal Military Academy. After graduation, he had some practical experience during the Napoleonic wars, but he was still undecided what career to follow when news reached him of certain interesting developments along the shores of the Rio de la Plata. He resigned his commission and went back to see for himself how he could be of use to the patriotic cause. This is what he found.

The city of Buenos Aires, then almost two and a half centuries old and since 1776 the official capital of the newly established vice-regency of the Plate River (that "Silver River" which is as muddy as the Mississippi after a spring flood) had become quite an important center of trade and culture. The vast cattle lands of the near-by plains were rapidly increasing the wealth of the Creoles, but like the native-born of every other part of South America, these good people were without any rights in the matter of self-government and had to accept a position that was hardly flattering to the pride of a race which was fully conscious of its own worth.

Therefore when Montesquieu and Voltaire and Rousseau began to talk of the rights of man, they had found a wide circle of eager readers among the younger generation of the Buenos Airians, who liked to hear these words, "The rights of man." As early as the year 1806 these revolutionary theories, poured into the form of concrete action, had caused outbreaks of open discontent. Being badly organized and as inexperienced in politics as their brethren of the north, the agitators for freedom had only succeeded in getting themselves shot and hanged.

But the scene had been changed over night when a British squadron had sailed up the River Plate and had used the quarrel between King Charles and his son Ferdinand as an excuse to attack this prosperous part of the Spanish colonies and perhaps annex it to the rest of Great Britain's possessions.

The Argentinians undoubtedly wanted to be free and they were more than willing to fight for their rights. But they were a proud race and, no matter what happened, they meant to be masters of their own fate. If they were going to be independent, they intended to establish their freedom by their own efforts and so they said firmly, "Thank you, but we don't want your assistance," to any one who meant to come to their help. They had little love for their Spanish oppressors but when the viceroy fled, as soon as a few British ships had been sighted, it was a small band of Creoles which organized the defences of Buenos Aires and drove the English away.

The next year, a second British expedition suffered a similar fate and the Argentine had been saved for Spain. But this victory had been the work of the native-born and not of the Spaniards. The royal viceroy had not dared to show his face in public until the last of the British frigates had disappeared and the role of his subordinates had been equally unworthy.

The native Argentinians had watched this cowardly behaviour on the part of their masters with increasing contempt and now that the danger was over, they hardly felt like returning to their former state of humble subjects. It was they who had saved the Argentine for Spain and they expected some kind of acknowledgment of their loyalty. When nothing was done to show that the Spanish Government appreciated their services, they resorted to action. They were so effective in the way in which they showed their resentment that the viceroy considered it the best policy to leave for home without bothering to say good-by to anybody.

He had one more successor, but the new representative of the royal majesty was no better than the old one had been. He talked only about his own rights and privileges until the exasperated Argentinians lost all further patience and sent the noble don a-packing with the request that he stay away for good.

During all this time, however, not a single word had as yet been spoken about national independence. Even when on May 25th of the year 1810 a *junta* was established to handle the affairs of the Argentine, everything was still done in the name of the King. But with the raising of a new Argentine banner, the familiar white and blue flag of today, everybody realized that the era of Spanish domination had come definitely to an end, and since that famous 25th of May of the year 1810 (the "Fourth of July" of the Argentine people), no foreigner has ruled over that part of the world and no foreigner is likely to do so.

When San Martin heard of the struggle that was going on in the old homeland, he knew the role he intended to play. He must devote himself to the cause of South American freedom.

It would take another volume to tell of this man's subsequent exploits on behalf of liberty. For the present purpose, it is enough to enumerate those which led to his historic meeting with Simon Bolivar, a meeting which was responsible for one of the greatest unsolved mysteries of history.

Two years after his return to his native land, San Martin was given the command of the armies of the Argentine and was told to carry the war into the enemy's territory. As his second in command, he chose one Bernardo O'Higgins, and the choice proved to be a wise one.

Bernardo O'Higgins, one of the three great figures of South American independence (Bolivar and San Martin were the other two), was the son of an Irishman by the name of Ambrosio O'Higgins, who had been Governor of Chile from 1778 until 1795 and Viceroy of Peru during the next six years. The father had taken an interest in the boy, although he had not been officially married to his mother, and as soon as he was old enough, had sent him to be educated in both England and Spain. Afterwards Bernardo had returned to Chile and had lived there peacefully until the outbreak of the revolution of the year 1810.

Successful in the beginning, this rebellion had run according to the usual pattern and as soon as a few successes had been gained, the leaders had started quarreling among themselves and the Spaniards had been able to defeat them in the disastrous battle of Rancagua in October of the year 1814. The defeated Chileans had crossed the Andes and had fled to Mendoza, where San Martin was busy drilling his troops in preparation for his forthcoming expedition against Peru.

O'Higgins and San Martin saw eye to eye and their cordial coöperation led to brilliant results. At the head of some three thousand soldiers and a thousand cavalrymen, they unexpectedly crossed the mountains and in the surprise attack of Chacabuco (in February, 1817) they destroyed the Spanish army which had been sent eastward to protect the city of Santiago. It was the cavalry of O'Higgins which had decided this encounter and San Martin, a fellow of generous gestures and willing to give credit where credit was due, eagerly supported O'Higgins when the latter took hold of the national government of Chile and became its first president.

In this way, the first part of San Martin's program had come to a successful ending. He now had to get ready for the second act and here he hit upon an entirely new idea. So far all the fighting in South America had been done on land but San Martin realized that he would never be able to get hold of Peru as long as the Spaniards were in command of the sea, for they could move their troops at will, while he himself had to march slowly through territories which had never yet been visited by a surveyor and where roads were as unknown as they were in the Scotland of the seventeenth century. And so he looked around for some one to provide him with a fleet.

He found this person in England. Thomas Cochrane, tenth Earl of Dundonald, hereafter referred to simply as Lord Cochrane, had been a brilliant officer in His Majesty's navy. Unfortunately he had also taken an interest in science. This had made him a suspicious character in the eyes of his colleagues, for British naval officers of a century and a half ago did not take much stock in such items as chemical laboratories and messy things in dirty looking bottles. We now gratefully remember him whenever we take a dose of bicarbonate of soda, but our grandfathers of a century and a half ago had never yet heard of this useful alkaline product. They knew about whiskey and whiskey was good enough for anything that ailed you.

Lord Cochrane therefore was left very much to his own devices and after his chemical researches had eaten up most of his fortune, he did a very foolish thing—he tried to recoup himself for his losses by speculating on the stock market. Being a novice at financial transactions, he soon found himself involved in a scandal. There was an investigation and there was a trial and although nothing was found against him, this distinguished officer was deprived of all his former ranks and titles and was reduced to such a state of poverty that he considered himself very lucky when he received an invitation from a revolutionary South American government to please come and help them build a navy. He was in command of the Chilean fleet from the year 1817 until 1822 and it was due to his excellent services that San Martin was able to blockade the harbors of Peru, while at the same time attacking the country from the land side.

In July, 1821, the Spaniards realized that they would no longer be able to hold Lima and they withdrew towards the mountains. San Martin thereupon proclaimed the independence of Peru and became the head of the first Peruvian Republic, with the title of Protector. He then prepared for a final drive against the Spaniards to clear the country completely of their presence and it was on this occasion that he came in personal contact with Bolivar.

I left Simon Bolivar a few pages ago while he was busy making a going concern of his newly established Republic of Greater Colombia. The southern half of Ecuador, which until then had been in the hands of the enemy, was ready to join him and so Peru remained the only country the fate of which still hung in the balance. The stage seemed set for a brilliant coup when news reached the Liberator that unless he hastened, there was a very good chance that Peru would be occupied by the troops of San Martin and would be forced to join the southern confederacy. The moment had come for quick action and Bolivar, who dearly loved the dramatic and the spectacular, did not mean to let it pass by without making a bid for success.

Early in March of the year 1822 he started for the south at the head of an army of two thousand men. In April he defeated the Spaniards in the Battle of Bambona. On May 24th, his second in command, the exceedingly capable Antonio José Sucre (like himself, a native of Venezuela) decisively beat the royal forces which had tried to halt him near the village of Pichincha, and the next day he occupied Quito.

These victories, while most welcome, only made the situation even more complicated than it had been before, because now one-half of Peru was in the hands of Bolivar, while the other half was occupied by the forces of San Martin. South America looked on with considerable interest, for here indeed was a problem of the first magnitude. Which of the two liberators was going to win out and get the credit for having set Peru free?

They could, of course, have ought it out on the field of battle, as had been done time and again by rivals for military glory. But this would have meant betrayal of those liberal principles upon which both had always prided themselves and such a solution was out of the question. There was only one other solution. They must meet each other and discuss the matter over a friendly glass of wine until they should have found a way out.

The result was the famous meeting of Guyaquil of July 26th of the year 1822—one of the greatest mystery-meetings of all time, for even today we are still completely ignorant about what was said or done on that occasion. Neither Bolivar nor San Martin ever revealed a word of

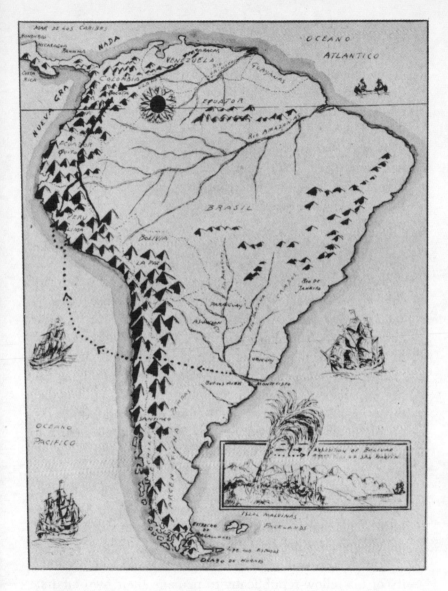

The race for Peru between Bolivar and San Martin.

what was spoken nor did either of them leave any notes or memoranda which could throw any light upon their discussion. After they had bade each other farewell (with many and highly effusive expressions of mutual respect), it is reported that San Martin had turned to the officers who were waiting for him, had sadly shaken his head and had remarked, "Gentlemen, this Señor Bolivar is not the man I had thought." But that story has never been authenticated and these words may never have been uttered at all.

Then what did they talk about during the forty hours they spent together in Guyaquil? There were then and there still are today a large number of guesses upon the subject, but only a few of them seem to make sense.

In the first place, there is a possibility that San Martin had suggested that Peru become a kingdom with the son of a European monarch as the head of the state. That, of course, did not mean that San Martin had gone back on his former revolutionary principles, but, like Bolivar, he must long since have come to the conclusion that the people of South America were as yet completely unfit for any kind of self-government. Better therefore, he may have reasoned, to train them for their independence under the leadership of some liberal prince of the blood than to expose them to an endless succession of domestic revolutions, headed by ambitious local politicians or military men in search of personal glory.

Bolivar also was none too enthusiastic about the ability of his fellow-republicans to manage their own affairs. But possibly he wanted to leave the "period of education" to the care of a protector or liberator (the name did not really matter) who had arisen from among the people themselves and so flatly refused to listen to San Martin's idea that Peru should be established as an independent kingdom. But I must repeat that all this is mere hearsay. For all we know, San Martin may never have made such a suggestion and it may have been Bolivar who talked of the chances of establishing a Peruvian monarchy.

Another possible reason for San Martin's hasty withdrawal from the scene has been found in the superiority of the forces that were at the disposal of Simon Bolivar, at least for the moment, as Bolivar was much nearer to his base of operations than San Martin.

But why go on? We don't know a thing about what happened during those two days except this: that the men met each other, that they had a long talk and bade each other farewell with at least an outward semblance of civility.

Yet something must have passed between them that was of sufficient importance to change the entire future of one of them. San Martin at the moment of that meeting was forty-four years old and he still had a long life before him. Why, at the height of his career, he should have suddenly dropped everything, should have resigned from the commandership of the army to go and hide himself in a little French town on the British Channel—all that constitutes one of the great puzzles of the last century. But that is exactly what San Martin did.

From time to time, when renewed outbreaks of political disorders seemed to threaten the independence of South America, he would offer to return and take charge, but he was never asked to do so. Another generation was arising and his name was rapidly being forgotten. Alone and on the brink of poverty (for he had been scrupulously honest in his political dealings), he died in the small French town of Boulogne-sur-Mer.

A strange man, I grant you, but also a great man, greater in many respects than Simon Bolivar. I know very little about him. I have seen his grave and I have read some books about him, but it takes more than that to get at a man's character, unless you are writing a modern book of "inside information," when a couple of hours in the city where his Aunt Doña Amelia lived will do wonders! As a mere guess, however, I feel inclined to say that San Martin was just a little too decent for the not very elevated business of making revolutions. One cannot be over-squeamish when one has to make decisions that may mean life or death to thousands of people. Bolivar, too, was not very good at that sort of thing. But on the whole, he was better fitted for the job than his famous Argentinian rival. And that may have been the reason he lasted a little longer, though it was a matter of only a few years.

In many respects, the year 1822 had been a good one for him. Among other things, it had brought him the news that the United States of America had at last recognized the independence of his Greater Colombia. But there also had been a great many developments to give him cause for worry. For one thing, he could never feel quite certain about those parts of the Republic where he himself was not actually on the premises. There still were groups of mountaineers who had remained fanatically loyal to their beloved King Ferdinand VII. There still were a great many conservative landowners who hated Bolivar's name with a bitter hatred as that of the man who had set the slaves free and who had talked nonsense about the right of every common day-laborer to a little piece of land of his own. And there were certain higher dignitaries of the Church, to whom Bolivar remained the incarnation of all that was evil until the very end of his days and even beyond. Among the rural priests (many of them Creoles and Mestizos) there was considerable sympathy for the cause of freedom but they had to proceed carefully and they took their risks when they agitated openly for the ideas and ideals of the Liberator.

What of the military situation? Spain had ruled over all this land for a great many centuries. Such a power does not disappear over night. It was said (but nobody knew anything for certain) that quite a number of Spanish soldiers continued to live among the valleys of the mountains. Some put the figures as high as fifty-five thousand. That was, of course, a gross exaggeration, but there were enough to be a very serious menace, and finally it was reported that the Spanish commander in chief was gathering together all these forces on the plains of Junin to try his luck in one final and desperate effort. The battle that followed is unique in the annals of military history for it was a battle of swords. Not a single shot was fired and all the fighting was done with the swords of the cavalrymen. The South Americans proved themselves better horsemen than their enemies and the Spaniards were defeated. But they still had several regiments of infantry and so nothing was decided.

It fell to the lot of Sucre, the hero of the Battle of Pichincha, to finish the work of liberation. On December 9th of the year 1824, at the Battle of Ayacucho, General Sucre annihilated the last remnants of the King's might in the northern part of South America. Thirteen Spanish generals and more than three thousand men fell into the hands of the insurgents and Sucre expressed himself entirely correctly when, from the battlefield of Ayacucho, he wrote to his commander in chief and dearly beloved friend: "The campaign is finished. The independence of Peru and the peace of America have been signed on this battlefield and they have been signed forever."

Sucre, too, is one of those South American leaders about whom we in the United States should know a lot more than we do. At best, we associate his name with the Battle of Ayacucho, which means to South Americans what Waterloo means to Europeans, but we are shamefully ignorant of his general character, although he was "a man of virtue," as the Romans would have expressed it. He had every chance to establish himself as a liberator in his own name, but he remained scrupulously loyal to his old comrade, the great Simon. He died only a short time before Bolivar and his death was a blow from which Bolivar never recovered.

Sucre happened to be on a routine mission to inspect certain garrisons and while passing through a forest, he was killed by a group of unreconstructed royalists. Now that they could no longer fight in the open, they had taken to murder. The assassins were never detected. In a way, that was too bad, for the King of Spain would undoubtedly have been delighted to reward them most liberally.

Ayacucho made the Republic of Colombia safe from further Spanish attacks, but in the interior, conditions remained as unsatisfactory as before. In a fine outbreak of generosity, the Peruvians offered Bolivar a million pesetas as a token of their appreciation for his services. He not only refused this award but, he went further. He resigned all his offices and once more threatened that this time he would withdraw definitely from public life. But it was too late. He had reached that stage in the life of a successful man when he begins to think of himself as indispensable and when that point has been reached, he is lost. He will go on and on and on, and unless the Good Lord is kind to him and puts an end to his ambitions by an unexpected death, he is apt to undo all he has accomplished, because he did not know how to time his exit.

And so there will be one more and very sad chapter— a sad chapter of decline and decay. I shall give it to you but it does not make cheerful reading.

Chapter VI.

The Decline and Fall of a Great Man.

IN THE SPRING of the year 1826, Simon Bolivar decided to leave Peru to visit Colombia and from there he meant to proceed to Venezuela where conditions, as he had heard, left much to be desired.

From that moment on, his life became like one of those movies I remember from my childhood days, in which nothing was ever quite distinct, in which everything was always a bit jumbled, so that one could only guess at what was happening.

I wonder what Bolivar himself thought of all this. From the bitter remarks he made during the last days of his life, he must have been a greatly disappointed man. But we should remember that he was very sick and that he had been ailing for a long time and his hopeless despondency may have been the result of his physical exhaustion.

It was the year 1826. In the middle of November, Bolivar had paid a final visit to Bogota and from there he had hastened to Venezuela, where one of his former generals, José Antonio Paez, the former *llanero*, seemed on the point of declaring himself dictator for the purpose of taking Venezuela out of the Union of Greater Colombia.

Such a step had long been foreseen. José Paez had done very useful work during the war of independence, but he was a person without any intellectual background and totally devoid of imagination. His political views were summed up in his favorite slogan of "Venezuela for the Venezuelans!" He had a deep contempt for Bolivar's visions of a union of all the republics of both North and South America. Such fantastic notions were beyond his limited powers of comprehension and he was in a commanding position in Venezuela, with Bolivar way off somewhere beyond the Andes, chasing his foolish rainbows.

Here at last the chance came for which Paez had waited all these many years. He started a rebellion and tried to make himself Venezuela's dictator. But his curious Indian brain (both his parents had been Indians) had failed to fathom the feeling of gratitude and loyalty which still inspired the majority of the people towards their Liberator. When he discovered his mistake, he hastened to make peace and abjectly he threw himself upon the mercy of his dear old friend, the great and good general. As usual, the great and good-natured general fell into the trap. He pardoned Paez and let him go scot-free. By this stroke of his pen, he saved the double-crosser for a career that was not to come to an end until the year 1873. After a great many ups and downs and several terms as president of the United States of Venezuela, the old Indian died peacefully in his bed in Brooklyn, N. Y. He had been the executive of one of our sister-republics. We decided to honor him as such and Paez returned to his native land on board an American man-of-war.

The Liberator's leniency towards Paez had made him many new friends in Venezuela but the people of New Grenada felt otherwise. They accused Bolivar of treachery towards their common country and again there were hints that he would never understand anybody but his own people and that it would be better to recognize this fact and to let the Union of Greater Colombia be dissolved into its original component parts. That would remove a great deal of friction, for then everybody could once more shout, "Venezuela for the Venezuelans!" and "Colombia for the Colombians!" and "Ecuador for the Ecuadorians!" and "Peru for the Peruvians!" the way it had always been before. A common country was no doubt a fine idea, but the time was not yet ripe for such a step among a people who rarely looked beyond the confines of their native village.

Bolivar had now given the best years of his life to the cause of freedom and independence. He was a very tired and a very sick man and he had had enough. He wanted to be free from all further cares of state. He had had a noble vision of a united South America, but everybody seemed to want a divided South America. Why bother any longer? Why not let them go ahead and do as they pleased?

He took a formal leave of all the countries he had helped to gain independence. His name still carried weight wherever he went. There were flowers and speeches but also there was treason. In September of the year 1828, that same Francisco de Paula Santander, whose cruelty towards his prisoners after the Battle of Boyaca had so greatly disgusted Bolivar that he had almost ordered his execution, tried to murder the Liberator. The conspirators were a motley crew. There was Santander himself and a sprinkling of Colombian army officers and the editor of an anti-Bolivar newspaper and a Frenchman of vague antecedents and a few others. They hoped to slay the Liberator by the well-known device of inviting him to a masked ball where no one would recognize them when they made their attack and they could therefore hope to escape without being detected.

When this failed, because Bolivar didn't come to the party, they threw discretion to the winds and one night they rushed the sentinels of the government palace where Bolivar was staying, killed the officer on guard and made for the Liberator's room. Fortunately, the door was locked and Bolivar was able to jump out of the window, which was only a few feet above the ground. The conspirators, finding their victim gone, then started a systematic search for him through the streets of Bogota. This led to armed encounters between those soldiers who were still loyal to their former commander in chief and those who had gone over to the side of Santander. Bolivar, hearing the shooting and not knowing what it meant nor which side was winning, hid himself beneath a bridge. There he was found by some of his friends, who now carried him back in triumph to his palace.

The next morning the people of Bogota tried to make Bolivar forget his humiliating experience by a noisy manifestation of joy. But the harm had been done. The man who had given these people their freedom had been forced to flee for his life, like a common criminal who had escaped from jail. It was a pretty low business.

As for the conspirators, they were duly apprehended and all of them were condemned to death. Fourteen of them were shot, but at the last moment Bolivar hesitated to kill his former assistant, Santander. He sent him to prison and eventually let him go. Why shed more blood? Why do anything at all in a world in which nothing seemed to matter any more except peace and quiet and rest?

But how to find these, when there still were several things that absolutely had to be done, unless everything he had so carefully built up was to dissolve in chaos? There was an uprising in the region around Quito. Bolivar was obliged to suppress it with the help of several regiments of Colombian soldiers. It made him feel as if he were engaged in some kind of civil war and he loathed the idea of brother killing brother. Fortunately, he was not compelled to take a personal part in the battle. When he arrived upon the scene, the faithful Sucre had already defeated the forces of the Irishman and former Spanish officer who was at the head of this latest rebellion. As for the rebels in the other part of Peru and Ecuador, they were still so deeply impressed by the name of Bolivar that they surrendered as soon as he himself came within hailing distance and they could recognize the familiar figure in its old, threadbare cape.

The name of the next traitor was Cordova. He had gained great fame in the Battle of Ayacucho, when the

A comparison between the territories covered by George Washington and Bolivar and San Martin.

charge of his cavalry had turned a possible defeat into a certain victory. Too weak to march against him in person, Bolivar left the campaign to another but thoroughly loyal Irishman, a certain Daniel O'Leary. O'Leary did a first-rate job. He drove Cordova and his men into a *cul de sac*, destroyed their army and killed Cordova.

But now came the worst blow of all. Old Paez, the

originator of "Venezuela for the Venezuelans," had started on still another campaign to take Venezuela out of the Union of Greater Colombia. Hesitant as always to march against a former companion in arms, Bolivar asked Sucre to go and visit Paez and arrange for an amicable solution of their difficulties. This peace commission was not even allowed to cross the Venezuelan border and Paez started to raise an army to deliver the whole of New Granada from the "notorious tyrant," Simon Bolivar. That was too much for Bolivar's pride. He, the man who had set that whole part of the world free from Spanish misrule, now had to hear himself denounced as a "notorious tyrant."

It was at this moment of defeat and despair that Bolivar wrote the bitter words, "Indeed, those of us who have toiled for liberty in South America have but plowed the sea." And it was then (on April 27th, 1830) that he definitely withdrew from a world of which he had long since grown tired. Ten days later he started for the port of Cartagena. He meant to go to Jamaica and from there, he expected to proceed to Europe, where he would try to forget until death should deliver him from his sufferings. But when he reached Cartagena, he discovered that he did not have enough money for the passage. He had spent both his health and his fortune in the service of his fatherland and his fellowmen. Now he did not have the few hundred dollars he needed to pay his fare into exile. There was nothing for him to do but stay where he was.

He found a welcome in the home of a friend and there he intended to remain until he knew what lay in store for

him. He was now practically alone. Even the faithful
Simon Rodriguez, the companion of his youthful travels,
had wandered out of the picture. He had come back into
Bolivar's life after the Liberator had established his Republic of La Gran Colombia. Rodriguez, now an old man
but still as full of impracticable visions as ever, had suddenly reappeared upon the scene. He was delighted. Reason at last had triumphed! Now the moment had come
to perpetuate the virtues of natural man by the establishment of a general system of education and he, Rodriguez, was ideally suited to be placed at the head of such
an experiment. His grateful pupil had been unable to re-
fuse so humble a request and Rodriguez had been appointed minister of education for the territory of Bolivia.

Within a remarkably short span of time, he had succeeded in quarreling with all his subordinates. They
knew how much learning the Indians and the Creoles
who composed the population of the new commonwealth
were willing and able to absorb and they told Rodriguez
that he talked nonsense. In the end, even Bolivar had no
longer been able to maintain this strange pedagogue in
his elevated position, whereupon Rodriguez, in high
dudgeon, had betaken himself to Chile, where he died
at an advanced age, full of theories about "human per-
fectability" but still without a decent suit of clothes to
his name.

After Rodriguez had departed, there remained only
one close friend, Antonio Sucre. Then news reached Bolivar that Sucre, too, was gone, and that was the blow that
killed him. "I have scarcely enough breath left for the few

days I shall still remain on earth," he wrote to a friend, and he meant it.

The doctors, realizing that their patient was in the last stages of consumption, suggested a change of air. A ship was found to take the Liberator to the village of Santa Marta, also situated on the Caribbean but a little further towards the west and better protected against the cold winds that came down from the mountains. Bolivar was removed to Santa Marta early in the month of December of the year 1830. A private citizen by the name of Mier, who had a country house three miles away from the little town, placed his home at the disposal of the dying hero. A few of his former officers and a priest friend accompanied him on his last voyage and they did whatever they could to distract him and give him a new hope for the future.

They talked to him about his plans for the conference of Panama, which now at last was to become a reality. It was to be the first of those Pan-American congresses at which Bolivar had hoped to discuss his grandiose scheme for a Pan-American Union and for coöperation between all the free nations of the whole of the continent. Thus far, nothing had come of it, as only half a dozen among the South American republics had promised to send delegates and the United States had been extremely lukewarm.

The isolationists among our great-great-grandfathers had feared that such a union might force them to take sides in still further quarrels between Spain and her former subjects. When finally Congress decided to send two delegates, one of them most unobligingly caught the yellow fever and died of it and the other arrived too late to be of any use. As for the British Government, it never got beyond a vague promise to send that most useless of all officials, an "official observer," and in the end, it did nothing at all.

The Congress of Panama therefore accomplished nothing. But to keep the dying man busy with pleasant thoughts, his friends kept talking of it. Next time, perhaps, such a gathering of all the American republics would be a success, and more arguments of the same sort. But Bolivar no longer listened. He had made his peace with the world. Only one more thing remained to be done. He must also make peace with his God.

On the tenth of December, the last rites of the Roman Catholic Church were administered to the Liberator. When an American man-of-war happened to drop into the harbor of Santa Marta, the ship's physician was asked to come and enter into consultation with the French doctor, who until then had been in charge of the patient. Together, they might still be able to save his life. But they knew better. They could do nothing.

When Bolivar felt that the end was near, he sent for one of his officers and dictated a final message to his fellow countrymen. That document still exists. It concluded with these dreadful and tragic words: "If only I knew that my death would bring union, then I could go down into my grave with a tranquil mind."

The end came late in the evening of the seventeenth day of December of the year 1830.

When the French physician made ready to lay out the body, he noticed that the shirt which Bolivar wore (the only one he had) was badly torn. He was horrified. He offered to take off his own shirt and place it upon the corpse of the Liberator. One of the officers in the room, seeing what was about to happen, rushed to his apartment and brought a clean shirt.

And so this great apostle of liberty, the man who had sacrificed everything he had ever called his own, his life, his wealth, his happiness and health, upon the altar of freedom, descended into his grave in a borrowed shroud, and the indifferent soldiers who had been sent out to guard him during his final moments could not even throw dice for the possession of his last garment.

Epilogue.

"THOSE OF US who have toiled for liberty in South America have but plowed the sea."

If those words, spoken in the bitterness of his final defeat and loneliness, had truly been the summing up of his restless labors, the life of Simon Bolivar might well have been considered a hopeless failure. Whereas a single glance at the map of the southern half of our continent proclaims the glory of his achievements. Half a dozen free and independent nations, arisen from among the ruins of Spain's imperial ambitions, are surely a monument of which any human being might well feel proud. Suppose the man who bestowed them upon the world was himself condemned to die in poverty and neglect—what of it? Does it not stand writ in the annals of history that no greatness can exist which is not directly based upon suffering?

This may seem unfair, when we measure success by the standards of our humdrum every-day existence. But genius obeys different laws, its divine purpose to accomplish, and one of these I just mentioned: there can be no greatness without tragedy.

Suppose that Caesar had survived the Ides of March. Then what? He would have become dictator of Rome. He would have grown old and fat (he had been bald from the days of his earliest youth) and he would have settled down as a retired Roman general in a pleasant villa on the bay of Naples. There he would probably have spent his days, puttering away in his garden, re-arranging his memoirs and being hen-pecked by a young and shrewish wife.

Suppose that soldier told to watch the door to the presidential box at the Ford Theatre had done his duty and had prevented John Wilkes Booth from fulfilling his murderous mission? Then Abraham Lincoln might have lived to become a small town lawyer or a representative in Congress for one of the mid-western states, residing in Washington with a socially impossible wife and wondering how he could make both ends meet without falling for the tempting offers of those New York publishers who were offering him a vast sum of money for a book on the real inside story of the War of the Rebellion?

Or can one see Joan of Arc returning safely to her father's farm near Domremy and from sheer boredom after so many years packed full of adventure, accepting marriage with that peasant lad whom she had left so summarily to go to war.

The list is endless. If Simon Bolivar, that morning in Rome, had not dedicated himself to the purpose of delivering his native land from the Spanish yoke, and if his young wife had not died her premature death, what then? Undoubtedly he would not have been buried in a borrowed shirt. On the contrary, he would have become one of the richest men of New Spain. He might have played an amiable role in the local politics of Venezuela and been appointed a general of the local militia, wearing

Ever before him the vision of a United States of both the Americas.

a uniform, covered with almost as much gold as that of the Governor General himself. And his brood of sons and daughters would most likely have teased him endlessly to be presented at court in distant Madrid (a city and a court he hated) and to take them to Paris that they might visit all the best dress-makers and return to Venezuela to contract ambitious and advantageous marriages and he would probably have spent the final years of his life in somnolent dignity, fighting his worthless sons-in-law who were forever plundering him, and listening to the complaints of his wife who felt that she had been slighted at the last governor's ball. Whereas now his name has become a symbol—his deeds have entered into the folk-lore of an entire continent—the spot where he breathed his last has become a shrine to be entered with bated breath by all those who love liberty more than they love life.

We are not privy to the inner designs of the Almighty and it is better for us that we never should be, for then life would cease to be the magnificent mystery it has been ever since man, endowed with a will of his own, entered upon the great adventure of shaping his fate according to the best of his own little hopes and ambitions. But the record of the last four thousand years (all we know more or less definitely about our strange doings on this planet) show us the wisdom of that mighty command which ordains that greatness can only be achieved through nobly fighting the great fight for that which is good and true (and therefore holy), and fighting it to the end regardless of the chances of victory.

I once wrote a book about the greatest of my compatriots, a painter who ended his days in dire poverty, yet had bestowed upon this world such beauty as never before had been revealed to human eyes. And when the moment had come for him to close the account, he asked his only surviving relative to read him a certain chapter in the book of Genesis. And this is what she read.

"And Jacob was left alone; and there wrestled a man with him until the breaking of the day.

"And when he saw that he prevailed not against him, he touched the hollow of his thigh: and the hollow of Jacob's thigh was out of joint, as he wrestled with him.

"And he said, 'Let me go, for the day breaketh.' And he said, 'I will not let thee go, except thou bless me.'

"And he said unto him, 'What is thy name?' And he said, 'Jacob.'

"And he said, 'Thy name shall be called no more Jacob, but Israel: for as a prince hast thou power with God and with men, and hast prevailed.' "

And even so, Simon Bolivar, descending into his lonely grave, left all of us—whether we hail from the southern half of our continent or from the northern part—the undying inspiration that comes from the example of a glorious leader who fought the good fight until the bitter end, and who prevailed.